Poems and Translations

Poems and Translations

ROBIN FLOWER

THE LILLIPUT PRESS
MCMXCIV

First published in 1931 by
CONSTABLE & CO LTD

Published in 1994 by
THE LILLIPUT PRESS LTD
4 Rosemount Terrace, Arbour Hill,
Dublin 7, Ireland.

A CIP record for this
title is available from
The British Library.

ISBN 1 874675 32 5

Cover design by Tim O'Neill
Printed in Dublin by ßetaprint

Preface

THE present volume was first published by Constable & Co Ltd in 1931 with the following note by Robin Flower:

'These poems and translations are a selection from the too scant harvest of twenty years. They are taken from two published volumes: *Éire*, 1910, and *Hymenaea*, 1918; and from seven brochures printed privately for my wife at successive Christmas seasons: *Thanksgiving*, 1922, *The Leelong Flower*, 1923, *The Great Blasket*, 1924, *Monkey Music*, 1925, *Trirech inna n-En*, 1926, *The Pilgrim's Way*, 1927, and *Fuit Ilium*, 1928. The volume of Irish translations, *Love's Bitter-Sweet*, was printed at Miss Yeats's Cuala Press in 1925. Most of the poems, I hope, explain themselves. But it may be said here that the poem 'Fand' is based on the beautiful story of 'The Sickbed of Cuchulainn and the One Jealousy of Emer', which relates how Cuchulainn, when his divine love Fand had been taken from him by her husband Manannan, shook his mantle between them for forgetfulness.

I observe some defects here and there in the translations from the Irish, which date in the main from fifteen years ago, but I hope that it will not be accounted to me for cynicism that I have left them as they are, fearing that a too scrupulous scholarship might play havoc with the poetry.'

He was Deputy-Keeper of Manuscripts in the British Museum from 1929 until 1944 and known to generations of scholars and friends for his wide learning in classical medieval and modern scholarship. A life-long visitor with his family to the Great Blasket Island in County Kerry, he was expert in the history of Irish story-telling in the oral tradition and is especially remembered, among his many other writings, for his *Western Island* and his translation of Tomas O'Crohan's autobiography, *The Islandman* and also for *The Irish Tradition*, which is being published as a companion volume to this book of poems. He died in 1946.

The family and I are much indebted to The Lilliput Press for bringing the book once more into print.

PATRICK FLOWER

Contents

A Dedication   *page* xi
A Note on the Author *by Muiris Mac Conghaill*   xiii
Peregrinari pro Amore Dei   1
Saint Ite   3
The Charm   4
The Hedge-Schoolmaster to his Love   5
Fand   6
The Sidhe   9
Sea Children   10
The Nightingale   11
Joy's Immortality   12
The Apple Tree   14
Personality   15
Inscription for a Copy of the Song of Songs   17
On Ivinghoe Beacon   18
At Golder's Hill   20
The Pipes   21
The Fairy Wood   22
In the Train   23
The Vigil of Saint Venus   25
In Church   27
Creation   28
The Dead   29

MARRIAGE

If the fine needle-point of sense   33
Primavera   34
Hymenaea   44
Marriage   47
Beauty: A Sequence   48

THANKSGIVING

Love's Wing   *page* 57
Pyrrha and Deucalion   58
No Marriage   59
The Tree   60
Time's Fool   61
Love's Laughter   62
At Evening   63
In December   64
After Holiday   65
The Treasure   66
For the Children   67

MONKEY MUSIC

The Monkey Day   71
The Rebel   72
The Monkey Sailors   73
Ancient Wisdom   74
Man   75
Paripace and Paripale   76
Lullaby   77
The Wood beyond the Wood   78
The Moon Monkey   79
The Parrot   80
The Forest Ball   81
The Blooming of the Flower   83

THE PILGRIMS' WAY

The Pilgrims' Way   87
Tree Heresy   88
September   89
The Forest of Dean   90

Troy   *page* 91
Sketch for a Picture   92
At Bury St. Edmunds   93
Alone   94

THE GREAT BLASKET

The Passage   99
Tomás   100
Brendan   101
The Seal   102
Solitude   104
Poets   105
The Dance   106

TRANSLATIONS FROM THE IRISH

Invocation   111

TRÍRECH INNA N-ÉN

The Ivy Crest   115
The Scribe   116
Praise   117
The Lark   118
O King of Kings   119
Worship   120
O Christe Fidelis   121
St. Ite's Fosterling   122
The Ousel   123
The Tree of Life   124
The Good Man   125
The White Lake   127
The Wren   128
Pangur Bán   129

LOVE'S BITTER-SWEET

The Dispraise of Absalom   *page* 133
The Blackthorn Brooch   134
Death and the Lady   135
Haunted   136
Women   138
Speech in Silence   139
Light Love   140
Manus O'Donnell and the Earl's Daughter   141
The Free Lover   143
The Wise Lover   145
At Parting   148
The Proud Lady   149
Love's Bitter Sweet   150
Odi et Amo   151
Beware!   152
He Praises his Wife when she had gone from him   154
Two Ways of Jealousy   155
Diarmuid Ruadh Praises Beauty   157
The Curse   160
Sheila   162
The Honey Thief   163
The Cotter's Life   164
The Widow   165
Four Epigrams   166

FUIT ILIUM

The Flight of the Earls   169
The Exile   171
The Poet in Chains   174
The Censors   175
Epilogue   176

x

A Dedication

(TO BARBARA, SHEILA AND JEAN)

DEAR, yet more dear
For her by whose grace you are here,
Three lights of a continual year!

If in all three
(So diverse-humoured) be
Some wandering part of me:

Some purpose willed
But unachieved, some grace instilled
Into a dream that perished unfulfilled,

Some longing vain
And sweet survival of past pain,
Some hope too high for flesh to entertain;

All these if you
Have, you shall find joy all years through
Common as air and general as dew.

Give all to her
Who is Life's fullness and Love's harbinger,
Beauty unchanged while all things change and stir—

Beauty abiding
Calm above all deriding,
A moon behind all clouds serenely hiding;

A moon that still,
Hidden, has power to fill
Those clouds with all the radiance of her will—

And she will give
A charm to arrest the rapt and fugitive
Joy that shall live with you while aught may live.

The song I sing
Is as a bird for ever on the wing
Seeking a country of perpetual spring;

But be you bold!
And, happier-fortuned, you shall hold
For ever the bright wing, the notes of gold.

Then, if you go
This way or that way, you shall know
Nothing but youth that brightens, hopes that glow;

And men shall say
(Reading my faint songs by your valorous ray)
"This was the morning twilight of their day."

A Note on the Author

ROBIN ERNEST WILLIAM FLOWER (1881–1946) was born 16 October 1881 at Meanwood, Yorkshire. After a distinguished undergraduate degree at Pembroke College, Oxford, Flower joined the British Museum (now the British Library) in 1906 as an assistant to the Department of Manuscripts. He was to spend the rest of his working life in the Museum, becoming Deputy-Keeper in 1929 until his premature retirement because of ill-health in 1944.

Robin Flower was a scholar poet who lived out his five and three-score years in a rigorous journey to define the nature and terrain of the culture of the medieval world. Fortunately his journey took him to the heart of Irish culture both in its manuscript tradition and to that portion which survived miraculously in the Irish-speaking areas of the west of Ireland at the beginning of the twentieth century.

In 1910 Robin Flower came to the Blasket Island to study the spoken language and culture of the island community, having decided to complete the cataloguing of the vast collection of Irish Language manuscripts in the British Museum. This task had been commenced by Standish Hayes O'Grady (1832–1915), who was not been able to complete it because of illness. Flower

* Volume I of the *Catalogue of Irish Manuscripts in the British Museum* by Hayes O'Grady and Volume II by Flower were both published in 1926. Volume III (Introduction and Indexes) was published posthumously in 1953, and was revised and passed through the press by Myles Dillon with a preface by A. Jefferies Collins.

corrected and extended O'Grady's text, and catalogued the manuscripts for the second volume.*

Flower's undertaking was mammoth and necessitated him to learn Irish in its old, medieval and modern forms. His decision to go to Dublin in 1910 to study Old Irish, and thereafter to learn the living language, was crucial to the formation and elaboration of the mind of this most distinguished medievalist. His 'thorough knowledge of the literature of the Middle Ages', as his friend Séamus Ó Duilearga, founding-father of the school of Irish folklore, wrote at his death, 'enriched his sensitive appreciation of the unique character of early and medieval Irish literature, as also the orally preserved literature of the Gaeltacht which for Flower was part of the Irish culture-heritage—the unwritten counterpart of the literature of the Manuscript Tradition. His *Catalogue of Irish Manuscripts in the British Museum* will remain as an abiding epitaph to his learning, and to the humanity of his scholarship.'

Five other books contribute to that epitaph in their display of Flower's learning and humanity: *The Islandman* (a translation of *An tOileánach* by Tomás Ó Criomhthain [1936]); *The Western Island or the Great Blasket* (1944); *The Irish Tradition* (published posthumously [1947; reissued Lilliput 1994]); *Seanchas On Oileán Tiar* (1956) (lore from the Western Island—a collection of stories and other material taken by Flower in Irish from Tomás Ó Criomhthain and other islanders, edited by Séamus Ó Duilearga); and the present volume.

When Robin Flower came to the Blasket Island in 1910, he took lodgings at the house of Pádraig Ó Catháin, where John Millington Synge had stayed in 1905. Ó Catháin (Peats Mhicí) was the island's 'king'—*Rí an Oileáin*. Carl Marstrander, the

Norwegian linguistics scholar who taught Old Irish to Robin
Flower in Dublin, had lodged there in 1907 and suggested to
Flower that he might stay there also and meet the king's
brother-in-law, Tomás Ó Criomhthain, and perhaps learn mod-
ern Irish from him as Marstrander had done.

The young Flower's friendship with Tomás Ó Criomhthain
opened up to him the history and culture of the island and its
people, and the wider literary culture of Munster.

> He had lived on the Island sixty years
> And those years and the Island lived in him,
> Graved on his flesh, in his eyes dwelling,
> And moulding all his speech,
> That speech witty and beautiful
> And charged with the memory of so many dead.
> 'Tomas', The Great Blasket, 1924

The islanders befriended Flower and gave him a pet name,
Bláithín, from the Irish word for flower. *Bláithín* stepped into
the life of the island where to this day he is part of the collective
memory of the survivors of the Diaspora who now live on the
mainland facing the island, or at Hungry Hill in Boston, Mass.

The letters Flower received from the islanders for over forty
years are now among the Flower collection of papers kept in the
Department of Irish Folklore, University College, Dublin.

His published work on the Blasket island culture and litera-
ture, his British Museum Catalogue and *The Irish Tradition* pro-
vide an image of medieval and modern Gaelic-speaking Ireland
which is a primary source for all interested in a culture which
was dying when Flower first came to Ireland in 1910. His image
had informed generations of scholars and readers, and is an
enduring one unlikely to be replaced.

A Note on the Author

It is difficult to separate the scholar from the poet: there is a unity in Robin Flower's work, an ear for the music of poetry and an eye for the form of words: he wrote that 'to translate poetry by less than poetry is a sin beyond absolution'.

MUIRIS MAC CONGHAILL

Peregrinari pro Amore Dei

O IRISH dead,
    I reading in your ancient books all day
And every day
Yet never read
The inner secret thing they had to say.

You took by storm
God's kingdom brought so far from oversea
And with wild glee
Set shapes enorm
From your fierce hearts about the sanctuary.

Yet tender things
Among the looming shadows gathered round
And a sweet sound
Of many wings
Swept on the waters, trembled on the ground.

And the small beasts
That shun man's footfall in the woodland ways
Came to God's praise
And shared such feasts
As the rich forests yield in autumn days.

Here one would take
A fox, and one a deer for acolyte;
And fresh from night
The hawthorn brake
With you gave thanks in scent and song for light.

So beast and tree
And the dim fugitive shapes that gleam and hide
In wind and tide,
From air and sea
Spake to you secrets else to men denied.

Thus would I find
On the stained skins the lost and magic thing,
The eddying wing,
And in the blind
Branch-troubled glades the bird-voice quivering.

Saint Ite

Said Ite: "I will take nothing from my Lord save that He
give me His Son in fashion of a babe that I may nurse Him."
Then came the angel that was wont to do service about her.
" 'Tis good time," said she to him. Then said the angel to
her, "That thou askest shall be granted thee," and Christ
came to her in fashion of a babe.
The Comment of the Féilire of Oingus.

H<small>E</small> came to me
A little before morning through the night
And lay between my breasts until daylight.

How helplessly
Lay the small limbs, the fallen head of gold,
The little hands that clasped and could not hold.

I spoke no word
Lest sleep's light-feathered wing should lift and fly
From this low earth to that steep heavenly sky.

And when he stirred
And opened frightened eyes and called for rest,
I set him wailing to my maiden breast.

And thence he drew
With soft stirred lips and clutching hands that strove
Sweet mortal milk of more than mortal love.

When morning grew
Far in the East and the world woke from rest,
The King of Stars was quiet on my breast.

The Charm

THE West is behind me, the East before me,
  The North and the South to left and to right,
I bind to my charming the firmament o'er me,
  The hosts of the day and the hosts of the night.

The sun and the moon and the wrath of ocean
  And all things silent, all secret things,
The winds in their stillness, the winds in their motion,
  The flying wings and the folded wings.

I have burnt his hair in the hearth fire's burning,
  I have spoken the words that are ill to be said;
I have turned three times and three times turning
  I have cried the cry that awakes the dead.

And I know in the hut by the side of the river
  He wakes and wonders and feels the charms
Steal into his blood. He is mine for ever,
  Mine are his lips and his eyes and his arms.

The door stands open, the wide road calls him,
  His feet stir softly and take the way;
He comes by night—for a charm enthralls him—
  The road he never has come by day.

He comes, O God! there is naught can hold him,
  He feels my arms through the mist and rain
Cherish and claim and clasp and enfold him;
  He is mine and never his own again.

4

The Hedge-Schoolmaster to his Love

O DEAREST of dear ones, O sweeter than sweetness!
　Than the birds on the mountains more fleet in your fleetness,
With your hair on the wind like a stream of fine amber,
You came through the mist like the sun in September.

As I went at your side in the midst of your brightness,
Like a silver swayed birch was your lithe lissom lightness,
Your hand was in mine and our hearts beat together
And little we cared for the world and its weather.

Below in the town they were wrangling and brawling,
On the high hills of heaven the soft rain was falling,
The soft rain, the sweet rain, so silverly shining,
That it charmed us and lulled us till day was declining.

Then, hand clasped in hand, with a riot of laughter,
We ran to the town and the rain followed after,
Till he tired at the last of his splashing and streaming,
And the lovely lit stars through our window came dreaming.

Fand

QUIET he stood, and quiet lay
  The moving woods all round,
And the long grasses in the way
Stirred softly with no sound,
No voice of bird, no water's cry,
No windy whisper trembled by,
But in his brain a voice grew clear,
As of a presence wandering near,
Yet far away,
From some immortal atmosphere,
Some hidden day.

They shook between my heart and you
The mantle of forgetfulness
And sprinkled with an opiate dew
My consciousness,
But my poor heart remembers still
The impetuous heart, the fiery will,
The clear desire;
My beauty grown invisible
Still burns with fire.

They scattered dust upon my head
And walked the accursed and backward round
That set me with the living dead
And the lost people out of mind,
But I have found
No peace; and you shall never find
Peace in the music-haunted ground

Or in the whispering air,
Or where the moaning of the sea
Is lonely in the caves; or where
The mountain silence suffers me
In bodiless being still to be.

Go among men, and there forget
All that I was, put by the dream,
Sail on the unremembering stream
Of passionate deeds—and yet
In the mad height of war—or when
The bloody hunters gather in
On the struck beast—or where the gale
Shrieks in the straining shroud—even there
The very heart of joy shall fail,
The embattled spirit, bare
To the fierce lash of memory, quail
And I shall enter in,
Spirit with spirit endlessly at strife,
To find at last atonement of our sin
And change this life in death for death in life.
But this shall never be,
The changeless gods make firm the old decree;
They will not give again
To shattered hearts the old felicity
Or with new joy make void the ancient pain.

For these are very proud and very old,
How should the grey renew the golden hair
Or those most careless labour with our care
Or the spent heart cheer on the overbold?

These that have sundered me
From all the ways of flesh and the bright day
Know nothing of forgiveness nor can be
Subject as men to the compassionate sway
Of the relenting heart. We are bound, even we,
That are of the ever-living and know nought
Of the stern weight that lies upon the heart
Or the vast darkness shadowing human thought.

Yet we too have a part
In the necessity that hurries all
From darkness unto darkness. And so I,
Human for those sweet moons that knew my fall
And sealed me lifeless though I could not die,
Must hear the call
And go forth weeping to the weeping woods
And be a voice where voices else are none
And drift unseen about the solitudes,
Where once my eyes made merry with the sun
And my lips closed on lips that answered joy
With joy redoubled, all my limbs made one
Sweet music happy-hearted as a boy—
Now these things all are gathered to the past,
And you and I are twain,
Our bodiless wills surrendered to the vast
And impotent necessity of pain,
And on Time's littered and oblivious floor
Shall meet no more.

The Sidhe

We have no conscience and no care
  And us no sweets can cloy;
For we are of the ancient air
  And brothers born of joy.

We watch the earth-begotten men
  That still must dream and toil
Vainly, until they turn again
  Into their mother soil.

Light hearts are ours, light thoughts, light wings,
  And yet our songs can say
The secret of the elder things
  That men have lost for aye.

We have no conscience and no care,
  No trouble and no tears,
And yet we envy men that fare
  Sad through the saddened years.

Sea Children

I TELL you, men of Ireland, we
   Are of the people of the sea
And restless, wind-tormented still
Have no will but the water's will.

As the great sea-flood comes and goes
The tide within us ebbs and flows;
And high above us everywhere
Scream the wild gulls in the wild air.

They cannot cease, the lonely birds,
From moaning and the ancient words
That, heard but once by night or day,
Sweep the world's boundaries away.

These are the words that long ago
Were the interpreters of woe
To the sad queens and sorrowing kings,
That ruled above all human things,

Yet went forth wandering; and we
Are waves upon the self-same sea
That the winds lift a little space
Foaming and in a breath efface.

The Nightingale

WE heard the note
Of the last bells across the waters float;
The birds that sing
The silver secrets of the evening.

We watched the day
Pass far and far and very far away;
Saw from each farm
The silent smoke ascending into calm.

We watched expire
The fainting onsets of the waves of fire;
And, mist-enfurled,
The moon rose past the shoulder of the world.

Then loud and low,
Clear and confused, and strangely swift and slow,
We heard the wail
And passionate hunger of the nightingale.

He sang desire,
And all the darkling thickets thrilled with fire;
He sang despair,
And all the woodland wept and all the air.

And last the song
Soared in a rapture confident and strong
And was the call
Of Love triumphant always over all.

Joy's Immortality

THESE are the trees that saw them pass
   The happy fields among,
When they were only lad and lass,
   That now are dead so long.

When they were only lass and lad,
   The nesting birds would sing
As though their little hearts were mad
   With the new wine of spring.

And far across the wooded vale,
   How clear and sweet and strong
The love-bedrunken nightingale
   Would sing their mating song!

They saw the summer glories glow
   And rain of autumn leaves,
Nor wept that earth's own kind should go
   Where earth's own bosom heaves.

And they are gone! The trees remain,
   The birds are singing still,
The footsteps of the wind and rain
   Are silver on the hill.

But still I see them dancing on,
   The bridegroom and the bride;
The pained and mortal flesh is gone,
   The immortal joys abide.

Their eyes in every flower are glad,
  Their voice in every song,
As they were still but lass and lad
  That now are dead so long.

The Apple Tree

I AM the apple tree that stood
   Ere song had raised the walls of Troy;
Round me the shepherd folk renewed
   With every spring their piping joy.

My branches swayed with every breath,
   My wealth of blossom showering snowed;
They had no thought of pain and death,
   For life and joy unchanged abode.

But in a strange and shadowed spring,
   Sharp tremors ran through all my leaves;
Men came about me whispering,
   "Destiny some dark purpose weaves."

And as the year to winter turned,
   My leaves began to fade and fall,
A ruddy-golden apple burned
   High on the topmost branch of all.

They took the golden fruit away,
   And took the simple rustic joy:
Men come no longer from that day
   And I am lonely after Troy.

Personality

You have not been before
  And will not be again,
Not just that confident glance and spirit sure
  Nor cheek of just that grain,
Your stillness like checked speed,
  Your going like a spear,
Quick eyes and swift voice instant to the need
  And light laugh crystal-clear.

These things not Helen owned,
  Not she of Egypt, nor
That loveliness that the wise people stoned
  Lest it should bring them war,
Not whatsoe'er was sweet
  In the world's spring, or when
Summer and arduous autumn made complete
  All beauty among men.

And if before the end
  All lovely things were brought,
All perilous dreams great spirits had to friend
  Too high for human thought,
All the witched world found rare,
  All fire, all light, all dew,
All stars inhabiting the heavenly air—
  They would not make up you.

For still behind these things
  That are but as your dress
You hide in you and from your spirit's springs
  Feed that high loveliness,

15

Which having wrought, the gods
  Go sorrowing for Time's sake,
Who makes and in his hurrying periods
  Must all things made unmake.

Inscription for a Copy of the
Song of Songs

SOLOMON the king is dead,
Dreamless lies the dreaming head,
Gone the love and gone the laughter,
All but this that liveth after,
This that lives and laughs and lightens
As the spring-charmed blossom brightens.
Here a myriad voices sing
Like the dancing bells that ring
On the bridle of a king
Riding, riding over mountains,
Through the forests, by the fountains,
Till upon his questing eyes
Love's own garden shall arise;
Where the apple branches shine
High above the tendrilled vine,
And the cedar rising high
Lifts dark limbs against the sky,
And the pomegranate and pear
Shining fruits of sweetness bear,
Where the silver fountains falling,
Chime with birds that cease not calling,
And the sleepy pigeons brood
In a rich and gloomy wood.

Solomon the king is dead,
We are living in his stead,
And the birds and fruits and flowers
Of the garden all are ours,
And for all his kingdoms won,
Richer we than Solomon.

On Ivinghoe Beacon

THE Beacon over Ivinghoe
  Lifts up into the sky
A soaring shoulder out of earth,
  Where swift cloud-shadows fly
And winds in the bent grasses make
  A murmured minstrelsy.

There did we lie and watch at ease
  The armies of the spring
Across the winter-guarded vale
  Their gallant outposts fling
By Amersham and Aylesbury,
  By Wendover and Wing.

The Saxon and the Roman here
  These winds and suns have felt
And underneath this arch of sky
  At this green altar knelt
And the same night has gathered all,
  The Roman, Saxon, Celt.

I saw your eyes turn strange, your lips
  Were cold against my kiss,
And far behind your speech there dwelt
  Strange wavering mysteries
—The patient legions of the dead
  Spoke from their world to this—

And "Ah!" you cried, "you cherish now
  My beauty like a flower,

But how, when the soft graces fade,
  The magic lights lose power
And Time that did my body build
  Unbuilds it hour by hour?

"And will you, when deep winter chills
  The seasons of desire,
And love, the tattered balladist,
  Thrums on a ragged wire,
Past the grey hair and glazing eye
  Discern the hearted fire?"

*   *   *   *   *   *

Alone I climb the Beacon now
  And watch the world outrolled,
The farms, the fields, the breadth of sky,
  The wide unbroken wold,
And autumn's traitor banners hung
  Above the woods of gold.

It was my fault, that in Love's wells
  I troubled the clear springs
And, looking in his burning eyes,
  Recked little of his wings
And, being but a mortal made,
  Dreamed of immortal things.

At Golder's Hill

I SAW a child at Golder's Hill
Rule the wide kingdom of sweet will
And catch an innocent employ
From the abundant heart of joy.
He teased the mossy-antlered stag
And taught a puppy's tail to wag;
He made a playful ripple shake
The water-lilies in the lake;
Smelt at a rose, tiptoed to kiss
The over-arching clematis,
Ran shouting up the hill to stare
And watch the dying sunset flare;
Then from his calling mother hid
And would not answer when she chid.
So glad, he seemed no human birth,
But some wild spirit of the earth,
Some rapture of delirious mood,
Not yet betrayed to flesh and blood,
But elemental, swift and free
As sunlight dancing on the sea.

O happy heart! could you but keep
Safe from the heavy mortal sleep,
Wherein we wander, having sold
A heavenly hope for earthly gold;
Then would your morning of delight
Reach far into the realms of night,
Rich with the rapture that uncloses
Your brother lilies, sister roses,
And take for its eternal treasure
This sweet simplicity of pleasure.

The Pipes

WITH the spring awaken other springs,
Those swallows' wings are shadowed by other wings
And another thrush behind that glad bird sings.

A multitude are the flowers, but multitudes
Blossom and waver and breathe from forgotten woods,
And in silent places an older silence broods.

With the spring long-buried springs in my heart awaken,
Time takes the years, but the springs he has not taken,
My thoughts with a boy's wild thoughts are mixed and shaken.

And here amid inland fields by the down's green shoulder
I remember an ancient sea and mountains older,
Older than all but time, skies sterner and colder.

When the swift spring night on the sea and the mountains fell,
In the hush of the solemn hills I remember well
The far pipes calling and the tale they had to tell.

Sad was the tale, ah! sad beyond all saying
The lament of the lonely pipes in the evening playing,
Lost in the glens, in the still, dark pines delaying.

And now with returning spring I remember all,
On southern fields those mountain shadows fall,
Those wandering pipes in the downland evening call.

The Fairy Wood

IT was the Fairy Wood:
We called it so, for all we knew of good
And beautiful and beyond belief remote
Dwelt in those brakes of foxglove and bright fern
Whose feathery birches seemed to poise and float
Over young grasses sung through by a burn
And birds made music in that solitude.

Not far away the tide
With the changing weather roared and moaned and sighed,
And that salt savour mid the branches hung
And that blue splendour flashed across the green
And sea-blue and leaf-green together clung
Inseparable, and the skiey blue between
Made a third rapture in that singing pride.

For colour seemed to sing
In that young shade and living light of spring;
And in the happy birds and chattering stream
And whisper of leaves and that sea-breathing voice
And winds that walked the pathways of my dream
And your clear notes that bade all these rejoice
Song seemed no less than colour on the wing.

In the Train

WHEN they got in
    I saw they did not care to have me there,
But just as I had marked the precious pair
I felt the train begin
Its two-hour journey. There we were, we three,
That awkward pair and me!
They sat down in the corner very prim,
A foot or two of seat 'twixt her and him,
And she looked out at the window, while he stared
At me, who dared
By some malignant scheme
To come between a lover and his dream.
She was a pretty little thing
As such things go, snub-nosed and quick of eye,
Bright-cheeked as though as yet Time's fugitive wing
Had touched her very lightly passing by,
But for the rest a slight enough affair
Made of the clay that serves for common ware.
And he—no finer earth
Had suffered in the furnace for his birth.
You might have picked the two
At any moment from the casual crew
That in a city goes
Along the street, and why none cares or knows.

Of course in such a case
One can't help feeling out of place,
Even looks are crimes,
And so I hid myself behind the *Times*
And let the idyll run out to its end.
One never does intend
To eavesdrop in these matters, yet, somehow,

Faced by the instant here and now
One listens—those can blame
Who've never done the same.
Well, reading blindly at the Births and Deaths,
I felt their hands touch, knew their separate breaths
Were drawing each to other.
And in them yearning knew the mighty mother
Weaving the spells that she has woven of old
Since first the palm tree shone with dusty gold,
Since earth first felt in earth
Move a twin rapture and re-echoing mirth.
This is her cunning who eternally
Must live in things that die,
Who is the wine in vessels basely moulded
And in scrawled notes the song delirious folded,
Who labours without end
And none knows whither all her labours tend.
It may be that to her
The very thrust and stir,
The pulse and eagerness of love,
Crowns all the centuries she strove
In fume and darkness till she moulded man
And the ascent began,
Life after life till life should bring to birth
A rapture not of earth,
A song of which the words are living men,
And as a poet's pen
Traces the crabbèd words that are
More musical than any singing star,
So she in these
Poor things of earth aims at such harmonies
As, to our ears not given,
Are all the music of the gods in Heaven.

The Vigil of Saint Venus

I WONDER where the gipsies keep their vans
When winter brings the snow and rain,
Till spring comes back and hung with pots and pans
And painted new they take the road again,
And all the gipsy children running
Will never leave reluctant passers-by,
Or in some roadside clearing down they lie,
Their wind-tanned nakedness luxuriously sunning:
And then they come as yesterday they came
And plant their booths and raise the roundabouts,
By day a riot, by night a flame,
Whose jangling music mingles with the shouts
Of happy children riding for a fall.
And yesterday we saw them all,
Fanny and I,
The shows, the Aunt Sallies and the coconut-shy,
And women out of Egypt reading fate.
Fanny had orders not to stay too late,
And so just as the sun was going down
We went the long way home by Badgers Wood,
And where the fir trees crown
The slope, dark green amid young green and brown,
Just there we stood
To watch the sky, and I made Fanny sit,
And sat down near, and gave the ribbon to her;
But though I spent my heart's whole strength to woo her
She wouldn't give me what I asked for it;
But off she ran and I was left alone,
And came back through the twilight and the spring,
And heard the last pipe and the drowsy wing
Of the tired birds, the sleepy monotone
Of a lost wind among the branches straying.

And in and out with these a thought was playing,
Old as the wind and young as this year's birds,
Haunting my senses, those sweet Roman words:

Young lovers love that never loved before,
And love-acquainted lovers love once more.
Love and the world were born at once in spring;
Now as the birds take wing
Love flies with them and weds them each with other,
And now amid the trees the mighty mother
Winds with deft fingers all her bowers of green,
And throned the woods between
—Their leaves by rainy kisses new unfurled—
She gives her laws to all the singing world.

So one by one I dreamed the verses over
And loved the long-dead lover
Who sang the spring these many springs ago,
And now in spring lies low,
And never wakes to see the world made new,
But his sad words are true:
By silence was Amyclae overthrown
And on my lips lies silence like a stone.

In Church

Forty years long was I grieved with this generation and said: It is a people that do err in their hearts, for they have not known My ways.

I OFTEN wonder did they know His ways
Who wrought this habitation for His praise,
And builded high their hope in soaring stone,
And lit the windows with that glow,
And led the traceries so,
Through many a maze of intricate branching grown
Into such forests as the archangels know,
And charged the carven screen
With joyous fantasies of the summer wood,
Leaves and quick birds and squirrels pert between,
And, over all, that rood
Where the sad Christ these many centuries hangs,
The tired head fallen low,
The pierced palms dragging on the iron fangs,
And sees the generations come and go,
And here and there a face looks up at Him
And sees the sad eyes dim
Above the incense and the prayers of men,
Then turns to earth again,
And his heart trembles and his senses swim.

Creation

"In the beginning was the word."
   Ah! that we poets understand.
Have we not heard
The armed archangels of creation stand
Trumpeting over chaos, and marked the surges
Of baffled night swell outward from the centre,
And the divine thought enter
And set the seamarks and the landward verges;
And the unwearied word swept on,
In great and small undeviating still,
And to its own high will
Wrought the great lights and starry benison;
And, by the heavenly influences warmed,
Earth, to that mating word a fruitful mother,
In her deep bosom formed
All creatures in their kind each after other:
The sudden grasses and the young vines creeping,
The flowers that stood erect to take the sun,
The swimmers through the maiden waters sweeping,
The multitudinous lives that crawl and run:
All with deliberate art
So exquisitely formed in every part
As though each meditated bone,
Each delicate vein, each sinew finely strung,
Were each a separate miracle alone
And from impassioned contemplation wrung.

The Dead

THEY had forgotten that for which they died,
 Ardours and angers, valiancy and pride,
The blows given for blows, the blood, the stench,
The grenade scattering death in the dripping trench,
The humming death and the droning death in the air
And the sad earth pitted and riven everywhere—
They had forgotten all; and now gathered together
Like flocks of birds fluttering in the serene weather
When the exhausted summer day draws to an end,
Enemy by enemy going as friend by friend,
Rejoicing and rioting there, truants from life,
Forgetting mistress and friend, children and wife,
Released from hate and love, mated or unmated,
Wondering at how they had loved, how they had hated,
Spirits alight and alert, circling and flying
Over death and life, being done with living and dying,
Being free of the flesh, glad runaways from that prison,
Eager for joy, avid of light, from slumber arisen;
So enemy going by enemy as friend by friend
In the level light of the quiet evening end
They flew and mounted and dwindled and so were gone.
And the night drew down and stars came one by one,
A wandering wind began to mutter and sigh,
And the earth lay lonely under a livid sky.

MARRIAGE

TO
I. M. F.

IF the fine needle-point of sense
That trembles at the touch of beauty were
Slave to the subtler influence
Of the steeled will, as some fond wise aver,
For you that point should vibrate all day long
And the clear trembling issue into song.

But now how idly wavering to and fro
Through East and West and South it seeks the North,
And, whithersoever those wandering circles go,
Comes but a soft confusèd muttering forth,
Not the clean praises of that beauty whence
Falls the wild light across my world of sense.

Primavera

I

Last night we heard the elements in pain
  Rage o'er the sanctuary where we lay enshrined,
The creeping murmur of the insidious rain
  And unavailing anger of the wind.
Yet what to us the thunder on the roof,
  Or the lashed windows wailing in our ears?
For in prophetic peace we stand aloof
  And look through tempest to the sunlit years.
Time and his wrathful ministers of storm
  Take arms against us vainly, for we know
That in the soul the things to be take form,
  And love stands firm though all the world turn foe.
Let us love on, and dream, nor be afraid,
For out of dreams and love the world is made.

II

O terrible world, that hast such store of pain,
　　Such dangers ambushed in thy waste of years,
Such sorrows showering like the winter rain,
　　And for men's thirst such bitter wells of tears!
Love's chronicles of sorrow have we read
　　And conned his weary precedents of pain,
How many longing lovers died unwed
　　And how young passion did with beauty wane;
Yet not the less we front the dangerous days,
　　Unbending and unawed as those of yore,
And confidently tread the ancient ways
　　With all of doubt behind, all hope before.
One wins the quest where all the many fail,
And many died that one might see the Grail.

III

Those morning lovers of the times of old,
  That first laid hands upon the wings of joy,
That found earth brazen and that left it gold,
  Wrought at the building that no years destroy.
'Twas Love that laid the bases, fixed the scope,
  And measured justly with his rule and line,
And they, his labourers, builded with their hope,
  Their dreams, their wonder and their tears divine.
So age by age the fabric scaled the skies
  With walls of silver and with towers of rose,
And chambers hung with woven tapestries
  Figured with all his raptures, all his woes;
And we within this fortress live, whereof
The builder and the architect is Love.

IV

Not the great morning with his flight of fire
  Or the king-eagle gazing in the sun
Outflies the upward wing of my desire
  Or clearlier lists Love's earliest orison.
Up from the region of forgetting night
  Love lifts me on, and ever as I climb
I watch within my widening scope of sight
  The long perspectives stretch of space and time.
There all the lovers of to-day's sweet earth,
  There all the hoarded joys of yesterday,
There the young heralds of to-morrow's mirth
  Raise one triumphing and accordant lay;
And the song's secret my purged ears discover,
Love's one same substance lives in every lover.

V

The stars are throbbing in the lucid sky
   With silver pulses restlessly astir,
And thin-drawn wafts of vapour wander by
   And fade and leave no witness that they were.
Of old the starry aspect gave presage
   Of motions stirring in the womb of time;
Men read the lettering of the heavenly page
   And, reading, shunned to fall or dared to climb.
But the one planet ruling our intents
   Is Love that burns, a steady orb of light,
Set far above the sphere of accidents
   And changing orbit of the hosts of night.
Shall not our joy be from their joys as far
As this our planet from their faithless star?

VI

O many a morning shall we see unfold,
  And many a night that takes the sun away,
Day's gradual growing of the grey to gold,
  Night's slow subsidence of the gold to grey!
Each day that comes is as a ship in flight
  From the far circle of the unknown sea,
That touches at our island of delight
  In the vast ocean of eternity.
And now their merchandise is sweet as spring,
  Now salt as bitter leavings of the wave,
But we will take the traffic that they bring
  And bless the hands that good or evil gave;
For one munificent day has given us more
Than all the evil merchants have in store.

VII

Look from the cliff, look out upon the sea
   That, coiling round innumerable isles,
Foams on the borders of infinity,
   Fretted with travelling storms and treacherous smiles.
Our ship swings at the anchor far below,
   With folded sails and silence round the keel,
Unwitting what strange surge her bows shall know,
   What shores her peering crow's-nest shall reveal.
Far off the islands in their locked lagoons,
   All surf-surrounded and inviolate,
Dream under larger suns and mightier moons
   Than light this idle country where we wait;
Let us with morning from the harbour sweep,
Our pilot knows the ways of all the deep.

VIII

They say the gods are to the woodlands fled,
   Or deep withdrawn into the heedless sky;
In solitudes and silence of the dead
   Lies disenthroned each slumbering deity.
But I have seen in many a radiant street,
   Through mists of morning or of evening gold,
A soundless vision borne on glancing feet,
   Love delicately going as of old.
For he was made alone of man's delight
   And follows still the crowded ways of men;
Altars of others crumble in the night,
   His with a kiss are builded up again;
And on those altars hearts instead of spice
Are made an offering and a sacrifice.

IX

Say not that beauty is an idle thing
   And gathered lightly as a wayside flower
That on the trembling verges of the spring
   Knows but the sweet survival of an hour.
For 'tis not so. Through dedicated days
   And foiled adventure of deliberate nights
We lose and find and stumble in the ways
   That lead to the far confluence of delights.
Not with the earthly eye and fleshly ear,
   But lifted far above mortality,
We see at last the eternal hills, and hear
   The sighing of the universal sea;
And, kneeling breathless in the holy place,
We know immortal Beauty face to face.

X

Ah! cease to sing. The heavenward flight of song,
    Limed by a mortal weakness, sinks to earth,
Into the drear infinitudes of wrong
    And sad impossibilities of mirth.
The veiled and awful night resumes anew
    Her territories in debate with day,
The grass is tingling with the earliest dew,
    The last flower folded, the last bird away.
And we, the trembling children of desire,
    Let us go too, but never to forget
How the sky filled with presences of fire
    That even after sundown linger yet,
And this my mortal music seemed as fair
As incense melting in a golden air.

Hymenaea

I

IF I with song could make your music more,
　Or with its rapture quicken all your joys,
Then would I summon from my singing store
　　The poise and counterpoise
Of rhythmic words made sweet with gathered lore
　　From all their past employs.

II

Would they but come, the coloured words and brave,
　Each murmuring of the hour that gave him birth,
How one was sad, one merry and one grave;
　　But all the sorrow and mirth,
Blent in a symphony, should be your slave
　　And sing the joys of earth.

III

And, as it sang, the world would be again
　As in the golden morning of desire,
When the first maiden loved the first of men,
　　And the first dawn shed fire,
And the young winds about their woodland den
　　Sang through the leafy lyre.

IV

There were no cities then, no smoky pall,
　No eager highways opening on despair,
No flame of lights when gracious gloom should fall
　　Through the dim evening air,
But gradual moons and timorous stars were all
　　That lit the secret lair.

V

Round them the forest wildernesses sighed
  Under the homeless winds that stir and stray;
Night-wandering owlets in the darkness cried,
      The panther took his prey;
They had no fear; Love's sheltering wings were wide
      And brought them safe till day.

VI

We cannot know their simple joys and sweet,
  Or of the brown leaf make the buds of spring,
For time has trampled with his flying feet
      The mouths that strive to sing
And bound with leaden vanities the fleet
      And heavenward-climbing wing.

VII

But the great world goes onward as of old,
  With moon and stars and nightly gift of dew;
The unwearied sun's munificence of gold
      Doth day by day renew
The fainting earth, that leaps from out the cold
      Unto her summons true.

VIII

There is a resurrection from the tomb
  Of years, the grave-clothes that our souls enmesh;
Each wakening day brings with it from the gloom
      Its dreams and deeds afresh,
Dreams that are deeds astir within the womb,
      Deeds that are dreams made flesh.

IX

Therefore, remembering all the weary change
    And heavy burden of our lifeless fears,
We yet have hope, and watch the morning range
        Above the mist of tears,
If haply, to our prayers no longer strange,
        She shall shine down the years.

X

I do not bid you rest. The field is set,
    The great battalions through the twilight move,
Each to his post. The call is chanting yet
        And we stand forth to prove
If good shall strike down ill in conflict met—
        And on our side is Love.

Marriage

Dear, we are younger and happier than that day
  When you and I and Love were left alone
And the world's laughter and sadness died away
  Into a rapt and exquisite monotone;
We have lived and striven, not songless in the strife,
  We have known good things and ill and either star;
We are younger than these lives born of our life,
  We are happier than these little laughters are.

For life has given us this good gift: to know
The harmony in difference and that strain
Of humours unresolved that keeps us two:
Two souls that with a separate radiance glow,
Not to one dullness fused; that still retain
This You and I not less than I and You.

Beauty: A Sequence

I

I DREAMED last night that you were dead,
And I stood there
And looked at that you left upon the bed
Which had been you, and where
The gods had spent their exquisite skill to make
A lovelier than their loveliest, and given
A star away to you, and for your sake
Had plundered Heaven.
And so, I thought, perchance they take again
The interest of their lending, and enrich
The eternal joy from Earth's unending pain,
And the great speech
Of the immortal symphony is grown
Complete and round for this one word alone.

II

I woke and you were there
In breathing stillness laid,
Nor yet might Death invade
The inviolate fortress ·Life had left so fair,
And my affrighted heart
Beat to a happier music and I knew
All the still rapture of the night had part
In this new gift of you.
We had robbed Heaven of light,
And, even as robbers hold
In timorous joy their stol'n and dangerous gold,
So I that night
Slept not again, but waked and wept to know
How near to beauty beauty's overthrow.

III

Swift! O, be swift
All birds of morning to call up the sun
Suddenly to uplift
Triumphing light and run
After the fainting moon that flies so far
And make a happiness of day
And wake the roses, star on star,
That dreamed the night away;
And, blackbird, tune the flute
That sings the clearlier in the morning dew
For the dark hours and mute
That prisoned your rich music all night through;
Be happy; day is breaking
And with her beauty all high beauty waking.

IV

Even as a weeping child,
Wak'd in the enormous night, sinks into rest
By the rich mother-breast
And overshadowing tendance reconciled,
So I, that felt so late
The shadow of that passing and had known
The darkness thrown
By the huge wing and pitiless flight of fate,
Now turn once more
To where Life laughs in sunlight and the Earth
Unbosoms all her lore
And garnered mirth,
Where you and I are moments in the song
That the dark undernotes but make more strong.

V

This I and You that clings
About our inner being, whence it came,
Born of what flame
We know not, native to what place of wings;
Some wandering chime,
Perchance, of music caught
In straiter bonds, or, as the wise have taught,
The coming of eternity to time.
And when the fetter falls
That holds us here,
If it be darkness and a shadowy fear
Or a bright air beyond these prisoning walls,
Till at the summons we arise and go
We shall not know.

VI

The poet of Ierne long ago
In such an autumn-tide as here makes gold
The woods outrolled
And hangs all trees with fruitage ere the snow,
He, whose sweet lips long time has stricken mute,
Called this the sorrow-season, for, he said,
Now that long since spring's delicate hope is fled
Earth sorrows under fruit.
Earth sad with all fulfilment knows the end,
And we that caught the spring
In a fine mesh of joy and had to friend
High summer's tarrying wing,
All Love's imperious vintage drinking up
Find sorrow in the cup.

VII

Before eternity resolved
In suns and moons to Time's slow pacing turned
God where he burned
Alone in his own substance intervolved
Was lonely, being all,
And going from himself, himself began
Time; and, the darkness heaving at his call,
He knew himself in man;
And the rich world was god and the high air;
All these of the one substance sundered long
Unto each other throng,
Yet suffer in division everywhere;
Not once alone God died,
But is in all things alway crucified.

THANKSGIVING

If words to you
Give any pleasure, here are words that do
No more
Than say again things said a thousand times before.

Love's Wing

IN all winged Heaven there is
No wing to match with this:
Those lift but air and brightness,
This lends to earthborn clay a lovelier lightness.

Pyrrha and Deucalion

THE white fog on the down
    Eats up the grass, the trees and that raw town
And leaves us sole of all the world. Why! thus
A lovelier world must take its rise from us.

No Marriage

WHERE is no marriage and no giving
   In marriage, what's the worth of living?
But, being married, dear, in Hell
With us 'twere well.

The Tree

Rooted in all we are and all we were,
Stablished in use and wont no storm can stir,
The tree of Love in leaf and flower and fruit
Stands, till Death lay his hatchet at the root.

Time's Fool

LOVE *is* Time's fool,
  The veriest dunce in all his noisy school:
Time on the board writes "Never,"
And the poor blunderer copies down "For ever."

Love's Laughter

KNOWING the inevitable and timeless wave
That whelms Time's sons, the foolish and the wise,
Love's lips are grave,
But O! the light of laughter in his eyes.

At Evening

DEAR, if it be our fortune both to reach
A quiet haven in calm autumnal weather,
We shall have much for memory, much for speech,
More for still thought together.

In December

I F we remember
Aprils and Mays in that last cold December,
There shall be still in those December days
Sunny Aprils, confident Mays.

The April violet
Perishes, it may be, with a less regret,
Foreknowing
Next year another violet breathing and glowing.

After Holiday

WHEN from our holiday we came
  You knelt and coaxed the sullen flame
In the damp grate whence fire had been
An exile that long time between
—For they too went with us, the sweet
Household gods of light and heat,
And left the lone house cold and still
Shivering in that unhuman chill—
But now light answered to your call,
Trembling on picture, chair and wall,
Making of damp, unhomely places
Warm shadows and bright interspaces.
So warmth and light and laughter came
Hurrying after the leaping flame
And, from our wandering home once more,
Half sadly I shut to the door.
Half sadly—for a thought had come
Between me and recovered home,
A sharp thought not all sad, that yet
Borrowed its keenness from regret
That this warm homely present made
Yesterday's present a past shade.
They were so sweet those days when we
Idled beside the autumnal sea
And watched the foam-flakes showering down
On tawny sand and shingle brown,
While, lingering in a misty sky,
Time's lenient wings beat softly by.
But now no more in time may be
The self-same shore, the self-same sea
Or the same self in you and me.

The Treasure

SOME to delight have set a measure
  Long since;
Drained the forgetful wine of pleasure
And, living, found life's hidden treasure;
But we, whatever the strange years bring us,
Shall find no end of the dreams that wing us,
But, with foot failing and hand that trembles,
Hair that no longer its grey dissembles
And ear dinning and eye blinded,
With body weary and weary-minded,
Stumbling on shall observe no measure
And, drunk with pleasure,
Seek and not find the bewildering treasure.

For the Children

Now cakes begin, and puddings come
  Blown on a wind of spices home,
Snapdragons wave their flaming wings,
And the bird of Christmas sings;
The bird of Christmas sings till dawn.
The curtains of the night are drawn,
Every chimney opens wide
And down the destined presents glide.
Under the chimney-pieces they
On hasty wings flutter away,
Each to his station on the bed
By dreamless or by dreaming head.

MONKEY MUSIC

TO

BARBARA, SHEILA, JEAN

AND

PATRICK

FROM WHOM I HAVE LEARNED

ALL THAT I KNOW

ABOUT MONKEYS

The Monkey Day

DECENT monkeys always do
What they are accustomed to,
Never change from day to day
One way for another way.
With the sunrise they awake
And their early breakfast take;
When elephants their trumpets blow,
To the water-hole they go,
Then with merry frisk and chatter
Through the jungle airways scatter,
Till the sun grows hot at noon
And the drowsy forests swoon
In a steamy mist of heat,
Then the monkey folk retreat
To the slumber trees and sleep.
(But beware, nor drowse too deep
Lest at evening you awake
In the embraces of a snake.)
When the sun begins to sink
Tail with tail they interlink
And gather to the council-tree
Where the royal chimpanzee
Settles each debated cause
According to the ancient laws
Made when drops of sacred blood
First gave life to monkey mud.
Then to their own trees they run,
On a sudden drops the sun
And the monkey day is done.

The Rebel

ONCE there was a monkey that
Found the monkey order flat,
Tired of doing every day
The same things in the same old way.
He would every sunset time
Climb and climb and climb and climb,
Till he trembled dizzily
On the top branch of the topmost tree.
There he'd hang, as I've been told,
And see the forest burning gold
Leagues on leagues of lighted wood,
Till the reeling distance blued,
Misty mountains on the sky.
And one day they heard him cry:
"Why should I stay sorrowing here?
All day long a calling clear
Haunts my ear,
Something farther than the far
Where the crystal mountains are,
Something higher than the high
Where the thin cloud sails the sky.
There this pain
Will no longer burn my brain,
I shall see
(Where the happy monkeys be)
What the dreams of night foretell
And with me it will be well."
Off he set
(Bah! Bah! Bah!),
But he hasn't got there yet
(Ha! Ha! Ha!).

The Monkey Sailors

THE parrots squall
  And the buffaloes bawl
And we, we all,
Swing and go,
Tail and toe,
Diddle-de-dee,
From tree to tree;
Scuttle in glee,
One after another,
Brother and brother,
Dancing, swinging,
Falling, clinging,
You by the hand,
I by the tail,
Like boats on land
We sail and sail,
And the leaves are waves on a green, green sea,
But there never was sailor so happy as we.

Ancient Wisdom

BEFORE he wanders in the wood
Every little monkey should
All the ancient wisdom gather
From the wise old monkey father.
Grey with forest years is he.
He sits upon the Loobah tree
And tells of times he used to know
Long and long and long ago,
When the nuts were twice as big,
Like an orange every fig,
And the milk of coconuts
Flowed through all the monkey huts.
Monkey babies in the wood
In those days were always good,
And all little monkeys did
What the monkey mothers bid.
But those times are very far
And the modern monkeys are
Fond of naughtiness and noise
Just like human girls and boys.

Man

Stop your larking, stop your mumming,
Stop catching fleas!
What's that noise, what's that coming
Through the trees?
Listen how
His foot cracks on that fallen bough.
See how straight he stands, and look!
Arms and legs without a crook.
Tailless monster! not a hair
On his body anywhere!
What a white and foolish face!
Take your place.
Quiet! quiet! softly shut
Both hands round the coconut.
He's nearer now,
Poise it deftly on the bough.
Not a sound!
Drop no leaf upon the ground.
Look! he's coming round that bush.
Hush!
If we can but hit his head,
He'll be dead.
So!
Let it go!
Smash!
Crash!

Paripace and Paripale

PARIPALE and Paripace
Lived on the borders of Chimborace.
Paripale
Had a ridiculous face
And a most ridiculous tail.
Paripace
Had a ridiculous tail
And a most ridiculous face.
Said Paripace
To Paripale:
"I like your face,
But I really cannot abide your tail."
Said Paripale
To Paripace:
"I adore your tail,
But I can't put up with so plain a face."
So they fought and fratched
And struggled and scratched
And bit and tore
Till never-no-more,
Where the forest clambers up Chimborace
Will you see the face
Of Paripace
Or the tail
Of pitiful perished Paripale!

Lullaby

Now!
  Wind your tails about the bough!
Tightly cling
While I sing
A sleepy, sleepy slumber-tune.
See, the moon
Silvers all the topmost leaves
And the web the spider weaves,
Glittering with silver drops,
Wavers on the palm-tree tops.
I have heard an ancient rune,
Thus it goes:
There's a monkey in the moon
Slips at night with stealthy toes
Down a silver spider-thread
To the bed
Of every monkey sleepy-head,
Whispers in the hairy ears
Of the monkey mothers' dears,
Then they dream of funny things,
Think that they have parrot's wings
And can fly
In the sky
Up above the trees on high.
When they touch the sky, they stumble,
Tumble, tumble,
Whirling round and round and round,
But before they reach the ground,
All the filmy slumber-veils
Wither from their eyes.
                        And now
They are hanging by their tails
To a softly swinging bough.

The Wood beyond the Wood

THERE'S a wood beyond this wood
  Where we go if we are good
(So the monkey parsons say
In the great tree where we pray).
There in sunlight stand the trees
Lost in green eternities,
And the spicèd breezes flow
Through the ages to and fro.
Nuttier nuts are there and fruits
Grown from more than earthly roots.
There immortal monkeys swing
On branches green with endless spring
And no monkey overbold
On those branches loses hold.
In that lovely wood shall we
Find the everlasting tree
And eternally together
Frolic in the windless weather.
But, if we are bad,
There's a forest drear and sad,
Where chill rains for ever pour
On a swamp without a shore,
Cold and hunger are eternal
And no nut has got a kernel,
Snakes and jaguars never fail
Nor the evil monkey-hater,
Throned upon his iron tail,
The eternal alligator.

The Moon Monkey

THERE was a monkey once,
  A dreadful dunce,
Who every night
Stared through the branches at the pale moonlight
And sighed.
O how we laughed to hear him when he cried:
"O moon, dear moon!
Stoop to me soon
And in your sacred silver wash me clean;
For I have been
Most miserable of all the monkey kind,
Flea-bitten, blind,
A shrivelled fruit upon a rotten tree."
What fun to see
His upturned eyes with white moon-blindness shining
And hear his whining,
His thin, thin voice in tears dwindling and dwining!

The Parrot

MY mother frequently averred
The parrot is a vulgar bird,
Feather flaunting, scrannel throat,
Squawking a senseless note.

In the green salons many-leaved
The parrot never is received;
He can't keep with propriety
The rules of good society.

And still I hate his crimson wing
And shudder when I hear him sing
His shrill, mechanical patter,
Not like good monkey chatter.

So one day I shall track and find him,
Softly, secretly come behind him,
And give his song a check
And wring his emerald neck.

The Forest Ball

Lum lum lum! Lee lee lee!
Beat your belly, chimpanzee,
That's the drum.
Lee lee lee! Lum lum lum!
Whistle, whistle, parrokeet,
Shrill and sweet,
That's the fife.
Fireflies, waft your fleeting lamps
High above the jungle damps,
All the humming forest life,
Tweedle, tweedle! insects all.
Lum lum lum! Lee lee lee!
Hear the call,
Monkey bands!
All take hands.
Tumble now
Off the bough,
Catch and tumble, catch and tumble,
Don't you fumble,
Clumsy little marmoset.
To partners! Set!
Gambol round
On the ground,
Now fly
To the sky.
Hurry, hurry.
Scurry, scurry.
Up, up, up! Don't mind the flowers.
Send the fruits
Down in showers.
Now the midnight owlet hoots.

81

From the palm-tree's feathery top
Drop, drop, drop.
Hark the dying of the drum.
Lum lum lum
And a failing melody
Lee lee lee.
Stop!

The Blooming of the Flower

PALLA Lalla Zook
     With a weary look
Peered upon his palm-leaf book
And said:
"Nigh a hundred years are sped
Since the blooming
And perfuming
Of the Leelong flower,
All the monkey folk are dead
That wantoned in that lovely hour."

"Palla Lalla Zook,
     Leave your palm-leaf book,
     And tell me where,
     Earth, sea or air,
     I can find that blossom fair."

"Past nine mountains
     And nine fountains
     And nine rivers
     Palely quivers
     The air
     Above the valley where,
     Like a dropt golden tear,
     The Leelong bud makes sweet
     The atmosphere
     Under the tempered heat
     Of the still afternoon."

Oh soon! soon! soon!
     I left old Lalla Zook
     And his weary look
     And his palm-leaf book,

And past nine mountains
And nine fountains
And nine rivers
I came where shivers
The opal mist-wreath round it,
And there I found it,
Like a dropt golden tear,
Soft glowing in its bower,
The Leelong flower.

I saw where it did lie,
And I became all eye,
Then when its scent uprose
Was nothing but a nose.
Here I take up my lot
The monkey folk forgot
And Palla Lalla Zook
With his weary look
And palm-leaf book.

THE PILGRIMS' WAY

IN MEMORY
OF
JOHN FREEMAN

The Pilgrims' Way

WALKING from Reigate where the Pilgrims' Way
    Leans steep against the hill,
White memory of a million feet gone far
To find another shrine than that they sought,
A deeper rest than in their wayside inns,
And a long darkness gloomier than their yews,
I chanced upon a wood,
A wood inhabiting a little valley,
Climbing the slopes with its adventurous trees
And scattering lonely birches here and there.
It was a summer morning of low sun
And mist half risen; and over all the ground
From blade to blade of the dew-sprinkled grass
Hung little delicate webs,
Tilted this way and that as the blades leaned,
Light floating carpets spread for fairy feet,
Grey fabrics million-diamonded with dew
And flashing with unnumbered fires. And suddenly
A thought thrilled in my brain: "Here, yes, just here
All those years gone those pilgrim feet went by
Brushing the morning's webs. Their happy faces
Shone in this light, their morning talk and laughter
Echoed among such lone, such clustered trees,
And, singing and shouting, they
Went up over the lip of this low valley
And set their faces to the hill,
And, treading that white trackway of the chalk,
They passed into the morning and were gone."

Tree Heresy

To J. F.

LOVER of elms, rightly you've sung
Those shallow-rooted and broad-flung,
Those myriad-branched, rough-rinded trees;
Yet have I dearer loves than these,
Tree-worship has tree-heresies.

Firs on a Highland mountain caught
In their sharp spines my budding thought,
That to sea winds bowed haughty necks;
And ah! how the golden sunset flecks
Slim birches by the Yorkshire becks.

These hedgerow elms above the stooks
Hear the harsh eloquence of rooks;
The whaup wailed long about those firs,
The seagull's cry was blent with hers—
Solitude's lonely ministers.

Still past those birches in my mind
The grouse whirls by upon the wind,
Still through the summer noonday wells
Drowsily in the moorland dells
Bee-music from the heather-bells.

Stately through all these southern shires
Wide elms whose leaves October fires;
With birch and fir I take my part,
Whose slenderer, sparse-strewn branches start
From roots struck deeper in my heart.

September

WE saw the Earth
    Drained of her summer, yet not turned to autumn;
And she was like a human mother, one
Dressing her children for some dance,
And half they wear the daily dress
And half the festal colours,
Red ribbon or golden scarf,
And this she tries and that
And ponders which most beautifully becomes
All that young beauty; soon they will be dressed
In a full splendour for that full delight,
After to lay them down
In an abandoned weariness,
Tired and pale in the pale sheets,
And slumber till night gives them back
All rosed to rosy dawn.
So Earth above her trees
Touched here with lemon, there with a crimson fire,
Yearned like a careful human mother, she
More rapt, more careful and more mother-souled.

The Forest of Dean

THE quiet congregation of the trees
   Awoke to a rippled whisper. The light-winged breeze
Brushed leaf against leaf, softly and delicately fingering
Silken beech and ragged oak leaf; and in the cool shadow
And wavering dapple of tremulous sunlight lingering
As weary of the hot gold glow of the buttercup meadow,
And renewing his strength in the cool green and still shade
Of the forest, deeper and deeper burrowing in
By pathway and trackway and green ride and arched glade
Over hyacinth and the white starred garlic and curled fern,
And dreaming in some unvisited haven to win
New life from the growing grass and rejoicing return
To sweep from hill to valley, from valley to hill.
The birds were still,
Only far off a cuckoo calling,
Drowsily and perpetually a far-off cuckoo calling.

Troy

I READ last night with many pauses
—For the flesh is weak though the spirit be willing—
A book I bought for a pound and a shilling,
"The Trojan War's Economic Causes,"
Till slumber at last through my eyelids crept,
And I let the book fall from my hands and slept.
Then, as the hours of the night grew deep,
A dream came through the passes of sleep
Of the silly stories of Homer's telling:
The press of the ships, the gathering hum,
Iphigeneia dying dumb,
The Greek tents white on the Trojan shore,
Achilles' anger and Nestor's lore,
The dabbled hair of the heroes lying
Mid the peace of the dead and the groans of the dying,
Hector dragged through the battle's lust,
The locks of Priam down in the dust,
Andromache's agony, Ilion's fall,
And, over all,
The lovely vision of naked Helen.

Sketch for a Picture

INCREDULOUS Endymion leans above
  All that moon-beauty flushed with sudden love,
Amorously to his young embraces yielded,
But the shamed eyes with one crookt white arm shielded.

At Bury St. Edmunds

A TOWER whose bell-voice left upon the air
A rippled after-music lingering there,
As though with Time Time's slave how vainly pleaded,
By love, sleep, death—rapt three!—only unheeded.

Alone

I AM alone, alone,
There is nothing—only I;
And when I come to die
All must be gone.

Eternal thought in me
Puts on the dress of time
And builds a stage to mime
Its listless tragedy.

And in that dress of time
And on that stage of space
I place, change and replace
Life to a wilful rhyme.

I summon at my whim
All things that are, that were:
The high incredible air
Where stars—my creatures—swim.

I dream and from my mind
The dead, the living come;
I build a marble Rome,
I give it to the wind.

Athens and Babylon
I breathe upon the night,
Troy towers for my delight
And crumbles stone by stone.

I change with white and green
The seasons hour by hour;
I think—it is a flower,
Think—and the flower has been.

Men, women, things, a stream
That wavers and flows by,
A lonely dreamer, I
Build and cast down the dream.

And one day, weary grown
Of all my brain has wrought,
I shall destroy my thought
And I and all be gone.

THE GREAT BLASKET

TO

TOMÁS Ó CRIOMHTHAINN

The Passage

THE dark cliff towered up to the stars that flickered
   And seemed no more than lights upon its brow,
And on the slippery quay
Men talked—a rush of Gaelic never-ending.
I stepped down to the boat,
A frail skin rocking on the unquiet water,
And at a touch she trembled
And skimmed out lightly to the moonlit seaway.
I lying in the stern
Felt all the tremble of water slipping under,
As wave on wave lifted and let us down.
The water from the oars dripped fiery; burning
With a dull glow great globes
Followed the travelling blades. A voice rose singing
To the tune of the running water and loud oars:
"I met a maiden in the misty morning,
And she barefooted under rippling tresses,
I asked her was she Helen, was she Deirdre?
She answered: 'I am none of these, but Ireland.
Men have died for me, men have still to die.'"
The voice died then and, growing in the darkness,
The shape of the Great Island
Rose up out of the water hugely glooming,
And wearing lights like stars upon its brow.

Tomas

I LOITERED there, and he
Built up the turf-rick with how careful hands,
Hands that had built a thousand ricks and now
Worked delicately with a deft unconsciousness.
Below us the Great Island
Fell with white-shining grasses to the cliffs,
And there plunged suddenly
Down sheer rock-gullies to the muttering waves.
Far out in the bay the gannets
Stopped and turned over and shot arrowy down,
And, beyond island, bay and gannets falling,
Ireland, a naked rock-wave, rose and fell.
He had lived on the Island sixty years
And those years and the Island lived in him,
Graved on his flesh, in his eye dwelling,
And moulding all his speech,
That speech witty and beautiful
And charged with the memory of so many dead.
Lighting his pipe he turned,
Looked at the bay and bent to me and said:
"If you went all the coasts of Ireland round,
It would go hard to you to find
Anything else so beautiful anywhere;
And often I am lonely,
Looking at the Island and the gannets falling
And to hear the sea-tide lonely in the caves.
But sure 'tis an odd heart that is never lonely."

Brendan

SOMETIMES I dream the whole rock-girdled island,
Adorned with the pale grasses and high ferns
And delicate faint-hued blossoms of the cliffs,
Floats insubstantial on the sea
Like the upthrust back
Of the huge fish Iasconius, where much-wandering
And far-adventuring Brendan held the Easters
Year after year of that long pilgrimage.
For this is Brendan's sea,
And yonder Brendan's mountain cloud-encompassed
Stands lonely in the sky;
And here he pondered over the strange splendour
That led him on, island to island, lost
In the vague, unpathed, unvoyageable sea,
Till in the twilight of the polar ocean
Huge ice-hills, ghostly in the ghostly sky,
Loomed over his frail boat,
And on one gleaming pinnacle there clung,
A chained and brooding shape,
Iscariot, caught one day's length out of Hell.

The Seal

THE little bay ringed round with broken cliffs
   Gathers the tide-borne wrack,
And there the islanders come day by day
For weed that shall enrich their barren fields.
Here, since the cliff-path gaped,
Cloven by the winter's wrecking storms,
They had gathered to remake the shattered way.
We idled as they laboured
With listless, laughing talk of that and this,
When suddenly a seal,
Rising and falling on the changing tide,
Lifted a dripping face and looked at us,
A mournful face more sad
Than the grey sadness of a moonlit wave.
We spoke, and in a moment it was gone,
And an unpeopled sea
Washed up and died in foam upon the shore.
Said one: "He's lonely after his brother still."
And so we heard the story,
A mournful memory of the island cherished
By the old dreaming people
And told round the dim fire on winter nights.
One twilight of late spring
The men had killed a seal out on the beaches
And brought it to a sea-cave for the skinning,
And, as they worked red-handed,
A voice out of the sea called "Brother!" once.
And then "Brother!" again. Then silence, only
A wind that sighed on the unquiet sea.

So standing in the surf
They saw as now a seal rising and falling
On a slow swinging sea.
They lifted their red hands and he was gone
Silently slipping into a silent wave.

Solitude

They could not stack the turf in that wet spring,
    And the cold nights were icy in our bones,
And so we burned furze and the rusted bracken.
I climbed the hill alone
And by the old fort gathered in the sun
Red fern and crackling furze;
And, as I worked, a mist came from the sea
And took the world away,
And left me islanded in that high air,
Where the trenched doon broods silent on the hill.
I do not know what shapes were in the mist,
But solitude was made more solitary
By some re-risen memory of the earth
That gathered round my loneliness,
And threatened with the dead my living breath.
I could have cried aloud for a sharp fear,
But the mist thinned and withered, and the sun
At one swift stride came through.
They passed, those shadowy threats,
And the great company of Ireland's hills,
Brandon and Slemish and the lesser brethren,
Stood up in the bright air,
And, on the other side the sea,
The illimitable Atlantic, rolled and shone.

Poets

SHE sat there, the strong woman,
　　Dark, with swift eyes alert and laughter-lighted,
And gathering that wild flock,
This on her knee, that at her side, another
Crouched hiding elfin-eyed under tossed hair;
A calf, unsteady-footed
And muzzled with a stocking, snuffed and blundered,
And chickens hither and thither
Pecked on the floor, fluttered on loft and settle.
"Poets? And is it poets?"
She said. "The day has been when there were poets
Here on the Island, yonder on the mainland.
And my own father's father
Was the chief poet of the Island. Wisha!
You'ld go to the well up there to draw the water
And talk a spell maybe, and come back to him
And he'ld have the poem for you, clean and clever.
He had the wit. If only he'd had learning,
Mother of God! 'tis he would have been a poet."

The Dance

ON the white wall flickered the sputtering lamp
   And lit the shadowy kitchen, the sanded floor,
The girls by the painted dresser, the dripping men
Late from the sea and huddled,
These on the settle, those by the table; the turf
Sent up faint smoke, and faint in the chimney a light
From the frost-fed stars trembled and died,
Trembled and died and trembled again in the smoke.
"Rise up now, Shane," said a voice, and another:
"Kate, stand out on the floor"; the girls to the men
Cried challenge on challenge; a lilt in the corner rose
And climbed and wavered and fell, and springing again
Called to the heavy feet of the men; the girls wild-eyed,
Their bare feet beating the measure, their loose hair flying,
Danced to the shuttle of lilted music weaving
Into a measure the light and the heavy foot.

TRANSLATIONS FROM THE IRISH

NOTE

THESE translations are of poems taken from the three periods of Irish Literature, the Old (8th-10th centuries, though the originals of certain poems, showing the same spirit, are of later date), the Medieval (14th-17th centuries), and the Modern (17th century). The first series has to tell of religious faith and the singing of birds, and has for a title Trírech inna n-Én, which means "The trilling of the birds," the second of love, and so is named "Love's Bitter-Sweet," the third of the fall of the old Irish order, and borrows a title from Virgil, "Fuit Ilium," for the destruction in the seventeenth century of Ireland as they had known it was to the poets as the fall of Troy. Some apology is perhaps necessary for the substitution of simpler English lyrical measures for the intricate and subtly interwoven harmonies of alliteration and internal rhyme in the Irish. But the attempt to borrow those qualities of verse could only end in a mechanic exercise, which might be a metrical commentary, but could not be poetry. And to translate poetry by less than poetry is a sin beyond absolution.

Invocation

Bards of the Gael, O sweet-lipped throng!
  After your race of music run
From that first morning hour of song
  To the red setting of your sun,

O disembodied spirits, come!
  Live, after centuries of pain,
Monk, noble, bard, no longer dumb,
  A moment in my life again.

From Alenn's hold, from Cashel's rock,
  From ancient Tara desolate,
From shores that take the Atlantic shock,
  From Ulster's mountain-guarded gate;

From Shannon's salmon-haunted wave
  And the sheer stream of Assaroe;
Where Erne's unwearied ripples lave
  Green isles; where Boyne's bright waters go;

Slieve Gullion's rocky fastness leave,
  Leave the stern hills of Donegal,
Mourne's veil that the salt sea-mists weave;
  Leave all the glens, the mountains all.

For there by river, lake and hill,
  I dream, through Éire's mortal sleep,
You cherish still your songs, and still
  Unchanged the ancient stations keep.

For with your love you clothed them round
  And told their secret legend o'er,
And, dying, left enchanted ground
  'Twixt Éire's seas from shore to shore;

And, riding by the bridle rein,
  You stayed the impetuous king, and told
The many-memoried tale again
  Of mount and lake and rampart old.

Whether in Éire's arms you sleep
  Or exiled in a foreign tomb,
That ancient trust you needs must keep,
  Love's strong compulsion draws you home.

And like the mountain plovers still
  You hover in the mists and call,
A wingèd song, a living will,
  O'er rath and loch and waterfall.

And I, whom eager love makes bold,
  Have sought where, after ages long,
Stained vellum and torn paper hold
  The hoarded treasure of your song.

I sing them in an alien tongue,
  And if, a recreant to my vow,
All over-harshly I have sung,
  Your pardon! O be with me now!

I would not stain your precious things
  Or do your holy memory wrong.
Make me a harp whose trembling strings
  Your ghostly fingers touch to song.

TRÍRECH INNA N-ÉN

Heaven's God, desiring
High, holy verse, remembers
My art, still on my lips inspiring
Song's golden embers.

The Ivy Crest

IN Tuaim Invir here I find
No great house such as mortals build:
A hermitage that fits my mind
With sun and moon and starlight filled.

'Twas Gobbán shaped it cunningly
—This is a tale that lacks not proof—
And my heart's darling in the sky
Christ was the thatcher of its roof.

Over my house rain never falls,
There comes no terror of the spear;
It is a garden without walls
And everlasting light shines here.

The Scribe

OVER my head the woodland wall
Rises; the ousel sings to me.
Above my booklet lined for words
The woodland birds shake out their glee.

There's the blithe cuckoo chanting clear
In mantle grey from bough to bough!
God keep me still! For here I write
A scripture bright in great woods now.

Praise

Lord, be it thine,
  Unfaltering praise of mine!
To thee my whole heart's love be given,
Of earth and heaven thou king divine.

Lord, be it thine,
Unfaltering praise of mine!
And, O pure prince! make clear my way
To serve and pray at thy sole shrine!

Lord, be it·thine,
Unfaltering praise of mine!
O father of all souls that long,
Take this my song and make it thine!

The Lark

Learned in music sings the lark,
  I leave my cell to listen;
His open beak spills music, hark!
Where Heaven's bright cloudlets glisten.

And so I'll sing my morning psalm
That God bright Heaven may give me
And keep me in eternal calm
And from all sin relieve me.

O King of Kings

O KING of Kings!
  O sheltering wings, O guardian tree!
All, all of me,
Thou Virgin's nurseling! rests in thee.

Worship

THE maker of all things,
  The Lord God worship we:
Heaven white with angels' wings,
Earth and the white-waved sea.

O Christe Fidelis

MY Christ ever faithful
With glory of angels
And stars in thy raiment,
Child of the white-footed,
Deathless, inviolate,
Bright-bodied maiden!

St. Ite's Fosterling

Babe Jesu lying
On my little pallet lonely,
Rich monks woo me to deny thee,
All things lie save Jesu only.

Tiny fosterling, I love thee,
Of no churlish house thou art;
Thou, with angels' wings above thee,
Nestlest night-long next my heart!

Tiny Jesu, baby lover,
Paying good and bad their due,
The whole world thou rulest over,
All must pray thee or they rue.

Jesu, thou angelic blossom,
No ill-minded monk art thou;
Child of Hebrew Mary's bosom,
In my cell thou slumberest now.

Though they come my friendship craving,
Sons of princes and of kings,
Not from them my soul finds saving,
But to tiny Jesu clings.

Virgins! sing your tuneful numbers,
Pay your little tribute so;
On my breast babe Jesu slumbers,
Yet in heaven his soft feet go.

The Ousel

I

THE tiny bird
   Whose call I heard
I marked his yellow bill.
The ousel's glée
Above Lough Lee
Shakes golden branches still.

II

He whistles in the willow tree,
Descanting from his yellow bill:
Gold-beaked, black-coated, that is he,
Stout ousel and his trembling trill.

III

Sweet ousel chanting blithely there,
Where in the bushes hides thy nest?
Thou hermit no bell calls to prayer!
Thy soft sweet music speaks of rest.

The Tree of Life

THE tree of life with bloom unchanged,
   Round it the goodly hosts are ranged,
Its leafy crest showers dewdrops round
All Heaven's spreading garden-ground.

There flock bright birds, a shining throng,
And sing their grace-perfected song,
While boundless mercy round them weaves
Undying fruit, unfading leaves.

A lovely flock! bright like the sun,
A hundred feathers clothe each one,
And pure and clear they chant together
A hundred songs for every feather.

The Good Man

This is the song the Devil sang to St. Moling

PURE gold, bright sky about the sun,
A silver goblet filled with wine,
An angel wise is everyone
That still hath done God's will divine.

A caught bird fluttering in the snare,
A leaky ship that wild winds shake,
A wineglass drained, a rotten tree—
Even such they be that God's law break.

A breathing branch that flowers in spring,
A vessel brimmed with honey sweet,
A precious ruby beyond price—
Such he that follows Christ's own feet.

A hollow nut that none desire,
A savour foul, a rotten wood,
A flowerless crabtree growing wild,
Are those defiled that Christ withstood.

The man that does Christ's heavenly will,
He is the sun that warms the year,
God's image through his heart doth pass,
He is a glass of crystal clear.

A racehorse straining for the goal,
Heaven is the mark for which he tries;
That chariot driven by a king,
A precious thing shall be his prize.

A sun that warms all Heaven round,
God loves him more than things of price:
A noble temple and divine,
A golden shrine of sacrifice.

An altar with the wine outpoured
Where sweet choirs sing in linen stoled,
A chalice with God's blood therein
Of findruine or precious gold.

The White Lake

WHEN holy Patrick full of grace
　　Suffered on Cruach, that blest place,
In grief and gloom enduring then
For Éire's women, Éire's men,

God for his comfort sent a flight
Of birds angelically bright
That sang above the darkling lake
A song unceasing for his sake.

'Twas thus they chanted, all and some,
"Come hither, Patrick! hither come!
Shield of the Gael, thou light of story,
Appointed star of golden glory!"

Thus singing all those fair birds smite
The waters with soft wings in flight
Till the dark lake its gloom surrenders
And rolls a tide of silvery splendours.

The Wren

WRENS of the lake, I love them all,
  They come to matins at my call;
The wren whose nest lets through the rain,
He is my goose, my cock, my crane.

My little bard, my man of song,
Went on a foray all day long,
Three midges were the poet's prey,
He cannot eat them in a day.

He caught them in his little feet,
His brown claws closed about the meat,
His chicks for dinner gather round.
Sure, if it rains, they'll all be drowned.

The crested plover's lost her young,
With bitter grief my heart it stung,
Two little chicks she had; they're gone,
The wren's round dozen still lives on.

Pangur Bán

I AND Pangur Bán, my cat,
'Tis a like task we are at;
Hunting mice is his delight,
Hunting words I sit all night.

Better far than praise of men
'Tis to sit with book and pen;
Pangur bears me no ill will,
He too plies his simple skill.

'Tis a merry thing to see
At our tasks how glad are we,
When at home we sit and find
Entertainment to our mind.

Oftentimes a mouse will stray
In the hero Pangur's way;
Oftentimes my keen thought set
Takes a meaning in its net.

'Gainst the wall he sets his eye
Full and fierce and sharp and sly;
'Gainst the wall of knowledge I
All my little wisdom try.

When a mouse darts from its den,
O how glad is Pangur then!
O what gladness do I prove
When I solve the doubts I love!

So in peace our tasks we ply,
Pangur Bán, my cat, and I;
In our arts we find our bliss,
I have mine and he has his.

Practice every day has made
Pangur perfect in his trade;
I get wisdom day and night
Turning darkness into light.

LOVE'S BITTER-SWEET

TO

TOMÁS Ó RATHAILLE

The Dispraise of Absalom

VEILED in that light amazing,
  Lady, your hair soft-wavèd
Has cast into dispraising
Absalom son of David.

Your golden locks close clinging,
Like bird-flocks of strange seeming,
Silent with no sweet singing
Draw all men into dreaming.

That bright hair idly flowing
Over the keen eyes' brightness,
Like gold rings set with glowing
Jewels of crystal lightness.

Strange loveliness that lingers
From lands that hear the Siren;
No ring enclasps your fingers,
Gold rings your neck environ.

Gold chains of hair that cluster
Round the neck straight and slender,
Which to that shining muster
Yields in a sweet surrender.

133

The Blackthorn Brooch

No rustic blackthorn brooch should rest
Above the shining of that breast,
Were there, O red lips of sweet sound,
But one gold brooch all Eire round.

Of fiondruine it should be made
The brooch that ties thy lovely plaid
Or marvellous pin of smithied gold,
Sweet singer! in thy mantle's fold.

Thy cheek's pale amber claims as right
A fair pin in thy mantle bright
Of golden or of silvery hue,
O thou most loyal heart and true!

Blood of my heart! I'd set no pin
That many-coloured mantle in,
O mistress of all hearts! but such
As showed the master-smith's own touch.

Death and the Lady

Lovely lady, rein thy will.
  Let my words a warning be,
Bid thy longing heart be still.
Wed no man. Remember me.

If my counsel like thee not,
Winsome beauty bright of blee,
Thou know'st not what deeds I've wrought.
Wed no man. Remember me.

If thou know'st not they are clay:
That slim form eyes may not see,
That round breast silk hides away,
Wed no man. Remember me.

Keep my counsel lest thou slip.
If love or hate men offer thee,
Hide thy heart and hoard thy lip.
Wed no man. Remember me.

Wed no man. Remember me.
I shall come thy joy to still
Though I shall not welcome be.
Lovely lady, rein thy will.

Haunted

Sweet lady, for thy honour's sake
Vex me no more, but let me be;
In life, in death, asleep, awake
Always I find no rest from thee.

A suppliant I with this one prayer:
Have pity nor beset me so
With that bright face and shining hair,
Where'er I stay, where'er I go.

Day and night I fly from thee,
But, whether long or short the way,
Those clustering locks, that step of glee
Follow me ever night and day.

O burning cheek! leave me to sleep,
Nor come in visions of the night,
And, when I wake, thy distance keep
And leave my staggering wits upright.

It breaks my heart to tell thee so:
Let my enchanted eyes go free,
And when death comes to end my woe
Stand not between God's love and me.

Of all God's creatures loveliest thou,
A wand his own hand trained in grace;
I never killed a soul, I vow,
Yet hast thou slain me in this place.

Out on thee! Thou had'st little need,
For, wert thou spiritless as I,
O crystal glance! O comely reed!
I had not doomed thee thus to die.

What shall I do to save my mind
That withers at thy lips' fierce fire?
Ah! take my blessing and be kind
And give me rest from this desire.

There's many a man that longs for thee,
Thy breathing lips and flesh in bloom.
Then, my heart's darling! leave me free,
Nor hunt me only to my doom.

Women

OF women no more evil will I say,
   The lightsome loves that help my heart to live
—The sun sees nothing sweeter on his way—
They pledge their faith and break it. I forgive,
All I forgive and scandal them no more.
I am their servant. Let the witless jeer.
Though their slain loves are numbered by the score,
I love them living and their ghosts are dear.
The cunning wits are loud in their dispraise,
And yet I know not. If their breed should fail,
What comfort were in all the world's wide ways?
A flowerless earth, a sea without a sail.
If these were gone that make earth Heaven for men,
Love them or hate, 'twere little matter then.

Speech in Silence

FIE on last night that sped so swiftly by!
 If I must hang, let me be hanged to-night.
Two in this house are speaking, eye to eye,
Though, lip with lip, they may not feed delight.
The jealous have no wit to interpose
In that eye-converse, whatsoe'er they do,
Our lips are silent and the watchers doze,
And eye to eye has passed the message true.
Dear, read my eyes across the jealous throng
There in your corner: "Keep this night for me,
Curse on the loveless nights that do us wrong,
Shut out the morn, curtain the night with thee."
Mary! slim queen of poets, hear my cry:
Fie on last night that sped so swiftly by!

Light Love

Out of sight is out of mind,
  Maids no loyal faith maintain;
Light love goes ranging and alway changing
Like a shifting April's sun and rain.

You were mine a year ago,
Love this year is fled away;
And that bright weather we knew together
Is clouded over since yesterday.

Ne'er a woman loves me now,
And my loving days are done;
That one should leave me it does not grieve me,
But women turn from me, every one!

Manus O'Donnell and the Earl's Daughter

I

LACKING the heart she stole, what shall I do?
Most pitiful of all things born I live,
Reft of my soul though all men else have two.
Ah! could I but for one swift moment give
To the Earl's daughter, she that wrought my woe,
This heart and its immedicable grief,
Then in her secret bosom would she know
Love's sorrow; and how barren of relief
Drags the long year; and with what fell disease
The sick soul tosses, day and night the same,
Feeding on grief since laughter cannot please
Until she give the heart back whence it came.
Unjust exchange! whereby my life's undone,
My true love hath two hearts and I not one.

II

Love is a sickness and a smart,
'Tis idly spoken:
He will not give me back my heart,
For it is broken.

O silly heart! to yield to Love
Yourself deceiving.
Your case can ne'er my pity move,
Since mine's the grieving.

Could I but hate who hateth me,
My freedom proving,
Since love is naught that I can see,
Or loved or loving.

III

My soul is full of bitter smart,
Our farewell spoken—
How many a fond and froward heart
Women have broken!

Like wanton tendrils of the vine
My grief is growing,
And dreams must mock this heart of mine
Now you are going.

But birds must leave their crystal spring
And suns their brightness—
With you, sweet, all my hope takes wing
And all my lightness.

IV

It ends to-night. All joy is hollow,
Fate takes the strong man in his mesh
And not the sun-god, even Apollo,
Could cure the canker in my flesh.

The whole wide sea of sorrow flowing
Brims all the harbours of my heart;
New pain on old for ever growing
Wakes to more woe the ancient smart.

Alas! 'tis truth the wise have spoken,
Wine has its lees and love can cloy,
And hearts too sorely tried are broken
And hollow all the hopes of joy.

The Free Lover

THEY lie who say that love must be
  A sickness and a misery;
He that ne'er loved woman knows
Never anything but woes.

I too love a woman; yet
My clear eyes are never wet;
Death has claimed me for his own,
Yet I live by love alone.

Clad in flesh and blood I move,
Though a swan-white maid I love;
Though I love I eat and sleep,
Music's service still I keep.

I'm no reed in water swaying,
My free thought goes lightly playing;
I'm no lover chill through all
The piled cloaks of Donegal.

I'm a man like others still,
Fires burn me, waters chill;
If the young and strong must die,
Ne'er so doomed a man as I.

Rope will bind me, this know I,
Like a sponge my mouth's ne'er dry,
Softer is my flesh than stone,
I can't drink the sea alone.

Though love within my bones doth play,
I know the night is not the day,
Black's black, white's white, a boat's a boat
And not a stately ship afloat.

I never call a horse a crow,
The sea's no hill, that much I know,
Small is less than great, I feel,
And a fly smaller than a seal.

Though I love her more than all
The sun-riped maids of Donegal,
Yet, by all the gods above!
I'm no sufferer for her love.

The Wise Lover

WE will not die, these lovers say,
   For any eyes but eyes of blue;
No hair shall win our hearts away
But hair of golden hue.

It is not with me as with these,
And yet a wiser song I sing,
Whom a love-lighted eye can please,
Black as the raven's wing.

I ask no roses in her face,
No golden shimmer in her hair;
A pallid cheek for me has grace
And jet-black locks are fair.

Dark was the mother of that maid
Who brought proud Ilion to its fall;
Yet shining locks of golden braid
Had Helen fair and tall.

Which was the lovelier of the two
—Red-lipped, sweet-voiced that winsome pair—
There was no man on earth that knew,
The dark one or the fair.

A tiny pearl men ring in gold
And little women I love well;
Of maids, hounds, horses from of old
Little are best, men tell.

I will confess to all around
That, since my heart to love inclined,
My worst sin is that I have found
All women to my mind.

For, be she little, 'tis no care,
Or be she tall, so love be fed;
A maiden young and straight and fair
Is fit for a king's bed.

There are whose skin as foam is bright,
Whose breasts are hills of stainless snow;
I love as well maids dusk as night
And girls of swarthy glow.

And be she sib to me, what care!
Or stranger from the isles of light;
A kindred maiden being fair
Claims love of double right.

Those witty women skilled to gloze
Their cunning favours I let pass;
A woman's wise enough who knows
What's clover and what's grass.

Widow or virgin, love ne'er cloys,
All charm my heart and this is truth;
A full-blown love has riper joys,
But beauty dwells with youth.

Whether in church or hall they move
With stately grace or modest charms,
They are dear, but dearest when their love
Grows wanton in my arms.

No beauty's counter to my will
Save when it's old and wrinkled grown
—And some are young at forty still—
Let each man love his own.

At Parting

FALSE love, since thou and I must sever,
   Hear this, the swan-song of my passion,
Let us be twain henceforth for ever,
Let thy heart follow my heart's fashion.

If thou shalt hear men speak about me,
If low or high scorn or befriend me,
Then leave them thou to praise or flout me,
Neither revile me nor defend me.

And if in church or cell thou beest,
In field enclosed or open meadow,
Whate'er I see, whate'er thou seest,
Let's turn each from the other's shadow.

Speak not, and I will speak them never,
Love-names or names our fathers gave us;
Forget as I forget for ever
How love with looking did enslave us.

The Proud Lady

How far apart are she and I!
I and the lady of my heart;
I yearn in love; she passes by
Too proud one kind word to impart.

For gold she left me here to moan,
Gold set her fragile thought astray;
But, came she in her shift alone,
I'd take her to my heart to-day.

How lightly on her spirit lies
The love that crushes my poor heart!
And, ah! she mocks my miseries.
How far are she and I apart!

Love's Bitter Sweet

SWEET is the pain
That lovers know,
Though never any
Hath told men so:
Love is, methinks, although it murders many,
The loveliest life God gives to men below.

The years in vain
Against him bring
Their archery:
Time has no sting
To wound his heart who loves. How should he die
Round whom a woman's arms their girdle fling?

Wide is his reign
That rules a heart:
There is no treasure,
No jewelled art
To win his eye, whose life swims in such pleasure,
Whose love is paid with love in Love's own mart.

Odi et Amo

Lo! I now hate that loved before,
And, lacking love, I cannot live.
If any after me adore,
To that crazed heart my curse I give.

Her gracious eye, her gold hair now,
Her voice—the bird's cry on the shore—
Her snowy teeth, her pencilled brow,
All these I hate that loved before.

Her crimson lips, her throat of snow,
Her hands, her speech—exhaustless store—
I would not that the people know,
And yet I hate that loved before.

Her name I will not hide away,
O, N, R, A, and one O more,
Read this my secret all who may,
For now I hate that loved before.

This woman pledged to me of old,
—Scarce one 'scapes scandal in five score—
I say, since truth must needs be told,
I hate her now that loved before.

Beware!

Lady! hearken. Say not now
   All thy heart dares to avow.
By thy curls, that golden clan,
Never trust a jealous man.
Say no word, but pass me by,
Tarry and keep a watchful eye.
Come not nigh me, speak no word,
In his own hour love is heard.
Little sparks make mighty flame,
'Ware the watchers of thy fame.
Sit not nigh me, dear one, so.
Jealous eyes watch where you go.
Sit not nigh me. Swift away!
Hear you not what all men say.
They are spying everywhere
On that bared head and bright hair.
While they watch our converse thus
Whispered speech is not for us.
Though it seem a little thing,
Touched hands might our ruin bring.
Since I may not hope for grace
Or leave to woo that winsome face,
Ah! why wed that sour one when
You had the choice of Ireland's men.
Every day I follow you,
Yet no speech between us two.
Rippling hair that wrought me wrong,
Fate has bound us in a thong.
Long the day for you and me,
Speech is bond if thought is free.
Thou whose ringlets curl and flow,
Life shall not be alway so.

On your lips a finger lay,
Doubt not love will find a way.
Hide thy captive heart from light
Like a robber in the night.
All the long day smiling be
Like a woman womanly.
Hard it is, yet silence feign
And, chief, that truant eye restrain.

He Praises his Wife when
she had gone from him

WHITE hands of languorous grace,
Fair feet of stately pace
And snowy-shining knees—
My love was made of these.

Stars glimmered in her hair,
Slim was she, satin-fair;
Dark like seal's fur her brows
Shadowed her cheek's fresh rose.

What words can match its worth,
That beauty closed in earth,
That courteous, stately air
Winsome and shy and fair!

To have known all this and be
Tortured with memory
—Curse on this waking breath—
Makes me in love with death.

Better to sleep than see
This house now dark to me
A lonely shell in place
Of that unrivalled grace.

Two Ways of Jealousy

I

THY wife is light, thou sayest. Well!
  Then heed not thou. This comes to all
And not alone thou walkest Hell,
Such rains on just and unjust fall.

How can she else? A woman she.
She heeds not now the cost and pain;
Love's hired servant must she be
And nevermore her own again.

Be wise in time and seeing see not,
Believe not half thy palsied fears;
Of proven things swear that they be not
And hearing hear not with thine ears.

Fond eunuch, go the way she's led thee
And nothing in the sun's eye see:
This the true wisdom shall bestead thee:
A blind and witless idiot be.

So at thy fill and soundly sleep,
Hide from her eyes thy torturing fire;
Take the two puddles at one leap
And fan the flames of her desire.

Whate'er she do, thou lov'st her still, such is thy jealous passion,
So fan thy wanton wife's desire in the true wittol's fashion.
But, if this thing thou can'st not do and honour still dost cherish,
Then like a madman fly away and like a madman perish.

II

O thou suspicion-mad!
'Tis an odd tale to hear;
No marvel thou art sad,
Yet there's no cause for fear.

A shapeless, grumbling wife
All wise men leave alone;
'Tis strange, but on my life!
Thy wife is still thine own.

Such cunning care as this
He chastity to shield
Guards beauty where none is:
A fence without a field!

One in a hundred here
Leads safe as thou his life;
Thou hast no cause to fear
Tongues scandalling thy wife.

Though all the world should come
To swear her life is bad,
Abide thou safe at home,
O thou suspicion-mad!

Diarmuid Ruadh Praises Beauty

I

The Lovely Lady

Sweet Jesu! was't to prove thy power or was it in repentance
For all the sorrows of the Gael under thy heavy sentence
That for the salving of their wounds thou sentest down from Heaven
This lightsome lady lovelier than the bright Pleiads seven?

For those rich tresses curl by curl gleam with a pearl-bright shimmer
And tremble still meandering down to where her white feet glimmer,
And there arrived they take no rest but turn and lightly springing
They soar towards her head again like bird-flocks upward winging.

And there her bright brows palely shine beneath that golden border
Where sunrays strive with lilied hues in strange and sweet disorder
And to that lovely lady's cheeks they lend a comely brightness
While the blood coursing neath her skin contends to flush their
    whiteness.

A magnet, sure, has touched her eyes, those keen and crystal lances,
For kingliest heroes fall a prey to their resistless glances,
And, though those veiled orbs seek the ground, 'tis only to dissemble,
A thousand hapless captive souls caught in their meshes tremble.

Her lips are sweet as honeycomb, crimson and fine and slender,
They close about her little teeth that gleam with pearly splendour;
And when they ope there issues forth a lightsome speech unbroken
As when touched lute-strings stir and tell their melodies unspoken.

Her neck is whiter than the swan that in the golden weather
Bathes in the foam of breaking waves her bright and downy feather;
There's nought to add or take away, 'tis perfect in its making,
For Christ's self wrought it straight and fair when she to life was
    waking.

Her sweet round breasts are virgin still, for no rude hand has
   smutched them,
Like whitest egg-shells newly laid that lie where none has touched
   them;
Her chaste and comely form is bright as may when spring winds
   fan it,
So slim, a baby's tiny hand, it seems, would all but span it.

All fever-wasted folk that long have lain in sorrow stricken
Till all their wits have gone astray in gloom no hope could quicken,
When cunning leeches all despair to heal their constant sadness,
My lovely lady passing by dispels the cloud of madness.

II

The Song of Thievery

Fair lady with the straight-ruled brows of strict and subtle weaving,
If thievery be counted crime and all that goes with thieving,
Methinks, thou comely countenance! 'tis likely thou wilt languish
For all thy plundered loveliness chained and condemned to anguish.

For, by my cloak, that golden hair with great eyes shining under,
So soft and long and curled and close, I swear it is but plunder;
If I have leave to speak the truth, that hair wherewith you queen it
Wrapped round the shaft of Cupid's darts erstwhile mine eyes have
   seen it.

And O! what theft was that in thee, thou sweet-lipped maid and
   sunny,
To rob the busy garden bees of their flower-gathered honey,
And then to set it in thy lips that I might sin with longing
To taste the swarm of kisses sweet in that rich garner thronging.

'Twas evil done to rob the bees, but worse remains behind it,
The charge of stolen stones of price proven the judge must find it;
The Ethiopian sought them out and ranged them in a cluster,
Thou stol'st and set them in thy mouth to lend thy lips their lustre.

Though all thy words are melodies in music softly flowering
And all men hang upon thy lips to hear those sweet songs showering,
I know not whence thou hast that spoil, what land of song thou'st
    raided,
Unless for lutes of English make that land thou hast invaded.

There's sorrow on the swan to-day unless thy spoil thou render,
For thou hast ta'en her snowy robe and all her downy splendour;
And O! the lily weeps to see her clear and sunny whiteness
Spread over those twin cheeks of thine in their unrivalled bright-
    ness.

Like the heaped winter snow that lies the Alpine mountains over
Twin breasts on that fair bosom swell and burst their jealous cover,
And all that sweet flesh over which thy sheltering robes are rangèd
The bright-skinned Daphne had it once ere she to laurel changèd.

But all, alas! amid those spoils each with the other vying
I saw my murdered broken heart, a hapless blood-clot, lying;
And yet it was no grief to him to count among their number,
Though night and day he tosses there unvisited of slumber.

Ah! lady, be not found in sin, if thou would'st be forgiven,
But yield up every stolen thing or e'er thou forfeit'st Heaven;
Yet if in unrepentant mood thou yieldest not thy winnings,
Then I forgive that crime in thee and all those lovely sinnings.

The Curse

*(Here is a poem made by a farmer of Fingal abusing
his nag because it threw him into a deep dirty pool just
in front of the girl he was going to court.)*

You brindled beast through whom I've lost her!
　Out of my sight! the devil take you!
And, 'pon my soul! this is no jest,
This year I'll rest not till I break you.

Satanic Ananias blast you!
Is that the way you learned to carry?
Your master in the mud to hurl
Before the girl he meant to marry.

The everlasting night fiend ride you!
My curse cling closer than your saddle!
Hell's ravens pick your eyes like eggs!
You scarecrow with your legs astraddle!

And it was only yesterday too
I gave the stable-boy a shilling
To stuff your belly full of hay
For fear you'd play this trick, you villain!

I gave you oats, you thankless devil!
And saved your life, you graceless fiend, you!
From ragged mane to scrubby tail
I combed and brushed and scraped and cleaned you.

You brute! the devil scorch and burn you!
You had a decent mare for mother,
And many a pound I've spent on hay
To feed you one day and another.

The best of reins, the finest saddle,
Good crupper and good pad together,
Stout hempen girth—for these I've paid,
And breastplate made of Spanish leather.

What's the excuse? What blindness caused it?
That bias in your indirections
That made a windmill of your legs
And lost for good my Meg's affections.

With my left spur I'll slash and stab you
And run it through the heart within you
And with the right I'll take great lumps
Out of your rumps until I skin you.

If ever again I go a-courting
Across your back—may Hellfire melt you!—
Then may I split my fork in twain
And lose the girl again as well too!

Sheila

That fresh face and tumbled hair
 Light my melancholy mood,
Though the people cry: Beware!
Wooing her you get no good.

Lose or win her, what care I?
Loveliness must needs be wooed,
Though the jealous people cry,
Though of her I get no good.

Though I get no good and woes
Dog my footsteps everywhere
Till about my pillow flows
All that golden flood of hair.

'Tis Sheila's back that puts the bards to rout
And her cold shoulder throws their music out;
I rush through madness to my soul's undoing
And yet I get no good of all my wooing.

The Honey Thief

Thou loveliest of all maids alive!
  Sweet robber of the wild bees' hive,
'Tis evil done, if thou art sane,
To make God's ordinances vain.

The Baptist had one meal a day,
The everlasting scriptures say;
In the Judean desert there
Honey and locusts was his fare.

From dairy, hive or church to thieve
Is sin no penance can relieve;
Sweet trickster! Heaven's honey eat
And rob no more that holy meat.

Though in thy lovely shining cheek the rose and lily vie
And by the sweetness of thy lips great warriors captured lie,
Thou harriest now the harmless bees, but one day thou shalt die
And a thousand bees on Judgment Day will hunt thee through the
  sky.

The Cotter's Life

A COTTER's life is hard. Who asks
To live that life has little wit.
For 'tis the worst of earthly tasks
To make a decent life of it.

With every rising dawn he sees
That all good things he must discard;
Hopeless he looks and finds no ease,
A cotter's life is bitter hard.

A skimpy grumbling idle wife
And many a sullen screaming brat
Ragged and foodless all their life:
A pleasant company is that!

This life has left me poor and worn and robbed me of my rest
And turned my stricken heart to fire and ashes in my breast,
And I that went so proudly once and laughed the world away
I curse myself and all my kind in misery to-day.

The Widow

He's dead and longer mourn him not
Since sorrow is the common lot;
We've heard thy tears of perfect moan,
So wed before thy beauty's gone.

Thou'rt not the only widowed fair,
So bless him once and leave him there.
Thy weeping will not bring him back,
He's dead. And men thou dost not lack.

Thou'st had—and counted small disgrace—
Much close play in a secret place.
Thou sorrowest for thy spouse, but he
Knew other women beside thee.

O lady that sheddest salt tears in a copious flow!
Cease wasting thy beauty, the truth of thy sorrow we know.
Other women are widows, thou art not the first or the last;
And, maybe, a new lover shall come e'er the month's end be past.

Four Epigrams

I

At Mass

Aʜ! light lovely lady with delicate lips aglow,
With breast more white than a branch heavy-laden with snow,
When my hand was uplifted at Mass to salute the Host
I looked at you once, and the half of my soul was lost.

II

Scandal

Snow-breasted star whose shining eyes are bold,
With ivory-gleaming teeth and locks of gold,
Mock not a sister fair who steers awry
Till thine own vessel in safe harbour lie.

III

Repent

Ah! golden girl so sweetly spoken
Let it not be charged on thee:
"She a Christian's heart has broken."
Repent and let love's fire burn free.

IV

A Vision of the Night

O chaste and fair! O sweet and rare! O slave of love and duty!
Whose clustering hair falls stair by stair down all thy house of beauty,
Thy shadow bright at dark of night went by where I was sleeping,
Thy form, thy face, thy peerless grace in slow procession sweeping.

FUIT ILIUM

Venit summa dies et ineluctabile tempus
Dardaniae. Fuimus Troes. Fuit Ilium et ingens
Gloria Teucrorum.

The Flight of the Earls

THIS night sees Éire desolate!
  Her chiefs are cast out of their state,
Her men, her maidens weep to see
Her desolate that should peopled be.

How desolate is Connla's plain
Though aliens swarm in her domain;
Her rich bright soil had joy in these
That now are scattered overseas.

Man after man, day after day,
Her noblest princes pass away
And leave to all the rabble rest
A land dispeopled of her best.

O'Donnell goes. In that stern strait
Sore-stricken Ulster mourns her fate
And all the northern shore makes moan
To hear that Aodh of Annagh's gone.

Men smile at childhood's play no more,
Music and song, their day is o'er;
At wine, at Mass the kingdom's heirs
Are seen no more; changed hearts are theirs.

They feast no more, they gamble not,
All goodly pastime is forgot
They barter not, they race no steeds,
They take no joy in stirring deeds.

No praise in builded song expressed
They hear, no tales before they rest;
None care for books, and none take glee
To hear the long-traced pedigree.

The packs are silent, there's no sound
Of the old strain on Bregian ground.
A foreign flood holds all the shore,
And the great wolfdog barks no more.

Woe to the Gael in this sore plight!
Henceforth they shall not know delight.
No tidings now their woe relieves,
Too close the gnawing sorrow cleaves.

These the examples of their woe:
Israel in Egypt long ago,
Troy that the Greek hosts set on flame
And Babylon that to ruin came.

Sundered from hope, what friendly hand
Can save the sea-surrounded land?
The clan of Conn no Moses see
To lead them from captivity.

Her chiefs are gone. There's none to bear
Her cross, or lift her long despair;
The grieving lords take ship. With these
Our very souls pass overseas.

Aindrias mac Marcuis.

The Exile

TAKE thou my blessing back again
  To Banba's wide and grassy plain
To the good friends of many a day
Who weep that I am gone away.

Be swift, nor dally anywhere,
Be sure they'll make you welcome there;
In Innisfail all love shall be
Thy guerdon for swift news of me.

Tell all that love me in the West
There is no trouble in my breast;
Whether on sea or land I go,
All good health and good hope I know.

In Éire or the West of Spain,
On mountains or the salt sea plain,
Where'er I go to-day, to-morrow,
Firmly I've closed the door on sorrow.

A fair wind sped us on our way,
So we came safe nor drove astray;
Only the best part of my sleep
I lost to hear the parson weep.

Killfree's good parson he was brave
As Connla once; but when the wave
Swept us by Rachly's Point he cast
All he had eaten first and last.

171

And when he heard the shrieking wave
And the chill waters past him drave,
O! how he longed to be once more
In Erris harbour by the shore.

And when an easy course we held
By coasts whence once Saint Brendan sailed
Alas for one in Sligo born
To toss upon the waves forlorn.

And as Kinsale we coasted by
The sun was shining in the sky;
Thirst's tortures would not let him be,
The parson was a sight to see!

He wailed in everybody's ear:
"I have no wealth, no children dear,
There's none to help me in the strife.
A parson's is a bitter life!

O! had I let the world go by
Like other priests that softly lie,
None in the West we leave behind
Had ever blamed me in his mind.

But now I shake with every breeze
On cold uncomfortable seas
And on the hatches toss in pain.
Good reason have I to complain.

In Coolavin had I but stayed
Where Tadhg O Higgin's scholars played
I'ld have slept sound, and never feared
To tumble as the vessel veered.

Fresh fish, fresh butter he'ld have found me,
A pillow and a blanket round me;
I was the master in that house
Where all the wandering bards carouse.

But no! I needs must run away
And God has punished me to-day,
The food I'll eat to-morrow's morn
A labourer at home would scorn.

My friend, I have no more to say.
I go on a wild road to-day."
A hundred leagues out in the sea,
The sickness passed and let him be.

Tadhg Ó Ruairc.

The Poet in Chains

WERE not the Gael fallen from their high estate
And Fola's warrior-kings cast down by fate
And learning mocked in Éire's evil day,
I were no servant, Edmond, in thy pay.

Ye shall not stay my toil, once held divine,
Thou and thy fleering harlots at their wine,
Till all the brave are dead, and out of reach
Éireamhón's people of the golden speech.

Edmond, I give good counsel. Heed it thou!
Leave mocking of my holy labours now,
Or such a rain of venomed shafts I'll send
That never a man shall serve thee nor befriend.

A tale I've heard that well might tame thy mood.
A gamesome chief of Gascony's best blood
Refused a poet once. The satire sped
And the man withered, strengthless, leprous, dead!

Peadar Ó Maoilchonaire.

The Censors

He told me yesterday, the friendly fool,
    News of that land where Conn and Corc held rule:
"The clerics frown on Gaelic's lightsome lays,
The legacy of the learning of old days."

I'll strive not now with them as once I strove,
When my adventurous wit was free to rove,
When every thought at once expression found
And my wit's weapons had an edge to wound.

The winged unerring shafts flew far and wide
And struck the niggard clerics in the side,
Rained on their tonsured crowns, while twixt the joints
Smote the keen venom of the glittering points.

I'll tie my lips together with a string
And count their miser's law a little thing;
And leave to God these who his gifts refuse
Who bind the poets and strike dumb the Muse.

Pádraigín Hacket.

Epilogue

Cáintear na fileadha
's ní hiad do bhíonn cionntach;
Ní fachtar as na soighthighe
acht an lán do bhíos ionnta.
Irish Epigram

MEN mock the poet for his want of wit,
Yet not the poet's is the fault of it;
Out of a little vessel you'll not gain
More than a little vessel can contain.